HAVE BATS, WILL TRAVEL

LIFE ON THE ROAD
with teenage baseball players

A TRUE STORY

JACK R. HELBER

STRATTON
—PRESS—
Publishing Life

Have Bats, Will Travel
Copyright © 2021 **Jack R. Helber**

Stratton Press Publishing
831 N Tatnall Street Suite M #188,
Wilmington, DE 19801
www.stratton-press.com
1-888-323-7009

ISBN (Paperback): 978-1-64895-431-3
ISBN (Ebook): 978-1-64895-432-0

Printed in the United States of America

This book is dedicated to all of the players who had the opportunity to participate with the Claremont Cardinals' American Legion baseball teams in the summers of their teenage years. The goal was to travel, see parts of the country, and possibly learn something while playing a game they loved. It is my thanks to them for making it possible each year.

INTRODUCTION

This is a twenty-year story about a traveling baseball team of teenagers. It is not about a specific team or an individual player, although they were part of the teams and part of the story. No player participated on the Claremont Cardinal American Legion team more than four years. This story is about an idea, a program for young men between fourteen and eighteen years old and the adventures they experienced while traveling away from home for a period of three weeks. Some players may be named, but I promised I would not use their last name, for their privacy. Prior to 1980, the Claremont Cardinals had been founded in 1972 but had never traveled in this manner before, and no one ever envisioned doing something like this for twenty years, but it happened.

The headlines read, "CLAREMONT CARDINALS GIVE AN EXTENDED DIMENSION TO AMERICAN LEGION BASEBALL!"

It started with a vision and a broken down school bus in 1980. Twenty years and tens of thousand dollars later, the Claremont Cardinals became one of the most admired American Legion baseball teams in the nation. Locally, this squad was the envy of every Little League player in the San Gabriel Valley. Dozens of hopefuls were turned away every summer at a chance to play for the Claremont Cardinals, whose 18 players ranged in age from 15-18.

What's the big deal?…an ordinary legion team was turned into a band of traveling teenagers that spends every summer taking its show on the road. (*LA Times*)

IN THE BEGINNING

S everal years ago, no one had ever heard of the Claremont Cardinals. Most people didn't even know where Claremont was (forty miles east of downtown LA), but we had gained a reputation, and not just because we've played well but because we haven't done the norm. We did not stay home. The major obstacle for this idea was, how would we pay for it? Each player was charged $500 to play, but we gave them ways to make that amount. Program ads was one of them. Part of that $500 would come back to each player through a daily per diem on the road. This was designed to give the players a little personal responsibility. Each player would get $10 a day for food or other personal expenses.

Another moneymaker was a free car wash. Now listen carefully, each player would be responsible for $1 per car washed. Find ten people to pledge 10 cents a car, and you have your $1. Get two locations in town, at a distance, run the car wash from 9:00 a.m. to 3:00 p.m. on a Saturday, and split the squad into two groups. At the end of the day, total up the cars washed, multiply that by the number of players, and add the donations from a jar set out as people drove in. That will raise a good portion of team money.

Finally, we had a Christmas tree lot for ten years. I owned an Orange Julius hamburger joint, and on the first week of December, I would open up a lot with trees from a reputable place, and I would use the players to work the lot on a schedule. In the first year, we netted $400, but as we got educated in the business, I think the last season we garnered $10,000. This went a long way in providing funds for the road.

A conversation with a cousin in Laramie, Wyoming, Paul K., while watching little brother Pete at Little League Playoffs in San Bernardino, eventually led to an invitation to play in a tournament in Laramie. This became our first traveling goal. Get to Laramie. But how? Eventually the transportation problem was solved when my dad spotted a used school bus for sale while on his way to work. We looked it over, and I bought it for $2,000, a 1956 long-nosed International Harvester school bus. We got help from parents in getting the bus ready to travel. One parent knew someone at an airport and also someone who could paint, so we took it to a local private airport and parked it in an empty hangar and had it painted team colors, a white bus with Cardinal-colored trim. Another parent helped us with some mechanical repairs, and several seats were taken out and replaced with a card table and beanbag chairs. We had some work done on the back tires and wheels. It was ready to go.

In a trial run, early in the season, we played in a tournament in Santa Maria, California, north of Santa Barbara near the coast. We took our "new" bus. We were housed at Vandenberg Air Force Base, which was a few miles from the ballpark, so we had a little ways to go back and forth. On one trip back from the ball game, cruising up a two-lane grade out of Santa Maria, all of a sudden there was a thud.

"What the hell was that?" I started to look back over my right shoulder and caught the sight of a tire passing us by the window of the door. Players were scrambling everywhere, jumping out emergency windows, throwing the back door open, and escaping out of the bus through it. Egad! The tire company had not tightened the bolts of the tires enough, and they worked themselves loose. Parents, who were following us back to the air base, loaded up the team and took them to our quarters. Damage was minimal, though, and we were able to put the tire back on the bus, limp it to a gas station, and have the bolts tightened down. After the tournament, parents drove the team home.

A few days later, Coach Greg and I hopped a short flight to Santa Barbara and picked up the bus. Hopefully, the bus was ready for the long road. Details of the journey had been ironed out. After several calls to teams up north, we were set. One of the players, Mike C., had contacts in Salt Lake City, and I had a brother who lives in a town north of Salt Lake. Between the two of them, we prepared the beginning part of the trip. My brother had arranged for gas stops on the way to SLC, which was a big help. He also made reservations for us to stay at Cherry Hill Campground in Kaysville, Utah, and a meal at Sills Cafe in Layton.

On a warm morning in June 1980, we all gathered at Memorial Park in Claremont, and our parents gave us a best wishes send-off to our first road trip. We headed to Las Vegas, where we were going to stop for a few hours. Most of the players hustled to the closest casinos to gamble. It didn't take long for them all to get thrown out for being too young, but they tried. First stop was Salt Lake City, Utah. This game was a disaster. It was a hundred degrees out, and the Utah team decided to beat the heat by removing their jerseys. This bothered me, because some of my players wanted to follow this bad example. No way! Act like a ballplayer! But I was worried that the rest of the trip would see some of the same things. We clobbered Salt Lake, 18–11.

The Cards leave Cherry Hill Campground Sunday morning headed to Yellowstone National Park. Crossing the border into Idaho on I-15, I realize I'm having trouble shifting to another gear. What now? When we bought the bus, I was told I would have to "double clutch." I had no idea what that meant, but played it off because I didn't want to appear stupid about driving. Of course, I had never driven a bus before. We get to Malad City, Idaho, and the bus is struggling. Actually, it is not going anywhere. We are in trouble! It is Sunday, this is Mormon country, where nothing is open on Sunday. After waiting around for a short time, a local resident stopped to see what the problem was. Another blessing, he knew the owner of an automobile parts shop in town. We met the owner at the bus. He recognized the problem, went to the shop, got the needed gears, and made the adjustments needed. I got the education I needed on how to "double clutch." We headed north on I-15 to Idaho Falls, where we exited onto US 20 to West Yellowstone, Montana. I found a campground, a KOA outside the park, and the Cards settled down for the night.

The next morning, we entered Yellowstone National Park. Several of our players had never visited Yellowstone, so this was exciting for them. Danny O., the spirited one, was playing catch with a Frisbee above the falls. It got loose and floated on down into the valley. I think it's still going. Visiting Yellowstone accomplished another goal of mine, play ball and see the country and its history. My fears were unfounded when we drove up to Cobb Field in Billings, Montana, for the second game on the trip. Billings, and Cobb Field, is a minor league affiliation for the Cincinnati Reds organization. We couldn't get out of the bus. It was Little League night, and all the Little Leaguers wanted autographs. This surprised most of our players because it was a new experience for them. Coach Greg had a Little Leaguer, with a wad of chew in his cheek, ask him for an autograph.

"Is that chew in your mouth?"

The kid answered, "Yep."

Greg asks, "How old are you?"

"Seven."

"Does your dad know you are doing that?"

The kid answered, "He's the one who gave it to me."

End of conversation! Greg signed the kid's ball. We finally got to the ballpark and the game. Big Mac pitched for us that year, and he went all the way to beat the Billings Scarlets, 9–2. We are on our way to creating a great program for American Legion baseball.

Our next stop, heading south or east on I-90, was Sheridan, Wyoming. The town is nestled under the impressive Bighorn Mountains of the Rockies. It is named after the Civil War Union general Philip Sheridan. We pick up a win, 12–4. From Sheridan, we continue on I-90 until it splits with I-25 at Buffalo, and we continue south on I-25 to Casper, Wyoming. We split a doubleheader in Casper, got up at six in the morning, and head for an afternoon game in the Laramie tournament. I-25 to a cutoff just south of Wheatland, where we will pick up Wyoming State Highway 34, and it will drop us off on US 287 south to Laramie.

Jim M. is our leadoff hitter in the first inning. He basically steps off the bus and up to the plate and hits a home run! "Yeah! Claremont is here!" We swept the tournament, including a no-hitter thrown by Big Mac against the hometown team, Laramie, and defeated a Colorado Springs Air Force Academy team, 9–3, for the championship. It was headlines in the local *Laramie Boomerang* newspaper. After Laramie, we headed home. But first, we had to find a "Husky" gas station to fuel up. The cry created by Mike M. was, "Find a Husky!"

The trip home from Laramie had its own adventures. To go west, we would have to cross the Rockies. I wanted to avoid that as much as possible in our bus. It was virtually impossible, but I thought I found a way. Stay east of the Rockies on I-25 and south, through Denver, Colorado, and further south, all the way to a junction at Walsenburg, and pick up US 160 to Durango. On the way down, we stopped at a campground out of Colorado City for the night. On this trip, we had saved a considerable amount of money by using campgrounds overnight. The bus was suitable for an overnight sleep, and the players were getting tired. This campground was right next to a railroad, and a seemingly busy one at that. At three in the morning, another train rolled through and blasted its horn (two long, one short, one longer!) That was it for Lefty, sleeping in the bus. "Nice campground, Helber!" He went off, of course waking everyone else. No one got back to sleep!

US 160 to Durango had its problems. We had to climb to 11,000 feet over a place called Wolf Creek Pass. It was slow going up the hill, and I was worried the entire time that we would heat up and boil over, although we had prepared with extra water. Heating up was not the problem. Altitude caused us problems with carburetor trouble. We were forced to stop dead on a two-lane road at over 10,000 feet, on a curve, to make a carburetor adjustment. The Claremont Cardinals had a shortstop, left fielder, pitcher, and designated hitter, etc., but we also had a designated mechanic on the team! I sent two players back around the curve to warn cars coming up, while the designated mechanic, Paul B., jumped into the engine and made the adjustment. It worked! We were on our way again to the top of Wolf Creek Pass and headed down to Durango. Let me say this, as a driver of a bus with eighteen young players, going downhill from 11,000 feet is more dangerous and worrisome than going uphill! We had one more overnight to make, and we did that at "Four Corners," where Arizona, Colorado, New Mexico, and Utah come together. It is on the Navajo Native American Indian Reservation. I pulled over to the side of the road, and we rested overnight. It was warm, so we put a couple of tents together and slept outside. Everyone got a chance to stand in four states at the same time.

We made it home on July 3rd, where one of our parents had entered our team, and bus, in the July 4th parade in Claremont. In 1980 is the last time I've been home on July 4th since. This was our first road trip, and after a slow beginning, it was a great trip. We were 11–3 on the road in games played and had tournament championships in Ogden and Laramie.

OGDEN TO YOUNTVILLE

The year 1981 was a banner year for the Claremont Cardinals. We played fifty-eight games and won thirty-nine of them. It marked the first time that the Cards played for the state championship—we'll get to that in a moment. It also gave us an introduction to a great Montana baseball town in Miles City. Once again, we sold Christmas trees to help support our coming summer season. And once again, the players would become involved in manning the lot. As Brad C., a transfer from Texas, reports, "I learned everything I needed to know about Christmas trees while selling them in the Orange Julius parking lot. I particularly remember the night sitting next to the Cardinal bus, playing cards on the picnic table, hearing on the radio, that John Lennon had been shot and later that he had died."

December and January are months that are usually used to schedule a summer season. I had conversations with coaches on our first trip and was told about a tournament in Miles City, Montana and that I should look into it, so I did. The tournament was in early July, and at that time they called it the Newhouse 10 Team Tournament. It was sponsored by the local beer-bottling company. It started on a

Tuesday, and the finals were on the following Sunday, so plan on being in town for a week. The fact that they would give us $1,000 to enter the tourney made the decision very easy.

The Newhouse was well organized and a lot of fun. Thursdays were an off day, whereby no baseball games were played, which allowed the pitchers a day of rest. However, it really wasn't an off day. Each team was to pick two players to represent them in a golf tournament beginning at 8:00 a.m. Each team was to pick two players to represent them in a bowling tournament at 11:00. One more team challenge called for four team members to pair up in canoe races at the local lake in the early afternoon. Points were awarded for placements in the tournament. These points were added to the evening activities. Two players from each team would vie for accuracy in outfield throwing, about two hundred feet to home plate. Each team would enter their two fastest runners for timing around the bases, and finally, each team would enter two players for a home run derby contest. This was exciting for me because I was given the opportunity to throw the home run derby! BP was something I liked to do. Before that event started, I got the hitters together and asked each one where they wanted the pitches located, to help me set them up. I wanted every pitch to leave the park! It was fun. The competition of the day gave several of your players a chance to participate in an activity. It also gave all teams an opportunity to interact with each other and, in many cases, make friendships from around the country. At the end of the festivities, the team with the total best scores in all the events was declared the winner. The entire day was exciting and sometimes raucous as the others on each team would attend the events and root for their teammates.

We entered the Newhouse Tournament for the first time. Now I had to schedule the rest of the season. Besides eighteen conference games, I had to make room for three tournaments down the road. On the 1981 trip, we opened up in Ogden, Utah, tournament. Next would be our first of nineteen years of showing in the Miles City Newhouse and ending again with the Laramie, Wyoming, tournament. In our travels, Interstates 15 and 90 were our main corridors to get around, so we headed up I-15 for Ogden, Utah, made a pit stop in Barstow, then headed north again.

A few miles up the road, we passed an off ramp for Zzyzx Road (not a misspelling). In the early nineteenth century, Spanish explorers and American Indians traveled the road to a mineral springs where the water was believed to have healing properties. Later, in 1944, the army named the road to Zzyzx Road, and it led to a popular health resort.

Baker is a small desert town below a mountain range and is famous in the area for two things. First is the "tallest temperature thermometer" in the world, reaching 134 feet into the sky. Second, for travelers, there is the "Baker Grade." After reading the temperature at over a hundred, we headed up the Baker Grade on I-15. Cresting the grade, we headed down toward Las Vegas. I suddenly realized we had no brakes! Holy moly! (You can read another four-letter word for *moly*.) We are headed downhill for seventy-five miles to Las Vegas with no brakes!

Quietly, I looked back to Coach Greg and said, "Greg, come up here."

"What's up?"

"We have no brakes, and I want you to come up here and sit on the emergency brake in case we need it."

We didn't tell the players, but they picked it up fast. I downshifted into low gear by double clutching, and between the gears and the emergency brake, we were able to safely get to Las Vegas. We exited at the Las Vegas Boulevard off ramp, and I immediately pulled over to the curb and managed to stop the bus. Just at that moment, a Las Vegas police car was rolling by. I hailed the policemen and told them of our plight. It was late at night, but I knew of a Shell gas station open all night on the strip, so I told the officer that that's where I was headed. With all the red-and-blue lights on the police car shining brightly, they gave us an escort down Las Vegas Boulevard. We didn't have to stop at one red light! We pulled into the overnight gas station and spoke to a mechanic on duty. They would look at it in the morning and determine what needed to be done. Now, what was I going to do with eighteen young men? Across the street was a Holiday Inn Express. We had reservations at a Holiday Inn in Ogden, Utah, so I talked to Vegas HI, and they called Ogden, and we changed our reservations to Las Vegas for no extra expense, five rooms.

Later, in the morning, I checked with the gas station mechanic about our bus. Bad news, he can't fix the problem for three or four days. Had to order a part. This made sense, because I wouldn't think that they would have a part for a 1956 International Harvester bus. After we get home from the road trip, Coach Greg and I will drive up to Vegas and pick up the bus and drive it home. But now what are we going to do? Two choices: abort the trip or form a plan.

I called for a team meeting in the morning. We all met at 9:00 a.m. in the Holiday Inn swimming pool. It was already hot, so that made it a great place. Abort was not an option! Okay, so let's get together and come up with a plan. Greg's brother said he'd drive a car up if we would fly him home. He did, we did. Big Mac's parents brought up their van, and we secured another vehicle. This will have to do. However, we would not be able to make the 5:00 p.m. game in

Ogden, so I called and asked if it could be postponed. Ogden gave us no mercy. We will have to forfeit. The players became very unhappy (there is another term for *unhappy*).

"Suck it up, boys, that's the way it's gonna be. We will just have to win the tournament!"

We did, by defeating Manhattan Beach, California, 4–2, in the championship game. That is what happened.

The Cardinals take the forfeit loss and then lose the next night to the home team, Ogden, 3–2, to officially start the tournament, 0–2. Not happy about that! We go on to sweep the rest of the way for the championship, including a 10–0 three-hit shutout by our little lefty with a big heart, Mike M. Our ace, Randy R., followed that up the next night with his own three-hit shutout, 3–0, with a little help from Big Mac's two-run home run in the sixth. (In American Legion, most tournaments were seven-inning games while conference games were nine innings).

It is in Ogden when we first play a team from Canada, the Lethbridge Elks. We will play them a few more times, including an invitation to their tournament, and it becomes the beginning of an international friendly rivalry. We also connect with a team from Las Vegas that we had met in Santa Maria. They wore all red uniforms, and we started to call them the strawberries. We will play them again in the next years, and the next time, at the ground rule meeting with the umpires, I will present them with a basket of strawberries. It was accepted with much laughter. In our first meeting against them afterward, we intentionally wore our all gold (yellow) unis and were surprised, at the ground rule meeting, when they took the opportunity to get even. We were presented with a bunch of bananas! It turned out to be a great relationship.

We stayed in the aforementioned Holiday Inn in Ogden. And while there, we had some interesting things occur. Danny O., our second baseman, had developed a unique mental regimen before he went to the plate to hit. He had an imaginary bird on his shoulder, and he quietly and carefully handed it to the next hitter on deck to watch it for him. The players got used to this, only to adopt it and play along with it for the rest of the season! They would gently hand it back to him when he returned to the dugout.

At the inn one day, Rob P. was spotted sitting in the doorway of his second-floor room and staring straight ahead.

"What's the matter with Rob?"

"He's homesick."

OMG! I don't have a medical cure for that! I attempted a short talk with him, with no response. His roommates had to sidestep around him to get into or out of the room. I told everyone to leave him alone, it will work out eventually. After about four hours, Rob seemed to snap out of his trance, but I think it took another baseball game for him to fully recover his emotions.

One morning at the Holiday Inn, I went to the candy machine down the hallway. Tried to put some change into it but couldn't find the slot. I stepped back to get a wide view and discovered the candy machine was upside down! What? My investigation, which was still going on after we left Ogden, found that Mark S. and Jeff W. had pulled the prank. A $10 per diem fine for both of them.

While in Ogden, my brother and his family scheduled a picnic for the team. What a great idea! So where should we go? We will go up the canyon near Farmington, to the "Towers." The towers were actually a radar station for Hill Air Force Base in Ogden, but they were at the top of Francis Peak, 9,560 feet elevation. The thrill was how you got there. We didn't take the bus! Drive up a narrow winding dirt road with at least 1,500-foot drop on the right side. It was scary, don't look down! It was slow going. We had fun at the top, picnicked, and made it back down safely. Before our Manhattan Beach game, we had scouted them in a prior game. At that time, we watched as they took their pregame warm-up. It was not your usual pregame. They put on a fun show of "Phantom Infield." This show was a pregame workout with *no* baseball—just pretend, with lots of individual ingenuity behind it. I thought it was great, and as a baseball coach who is ready to steal someone else's ideas, I noted it for further use at another time. We will address the Claremont Cardinal's "famous" phantom infield later.

From Ogden, we head out to Miles City, Montana, for the first time. We take I-90 through Billings until it veers south, and I-94 takes over going east. From Billings, we have 145 miles to go. The Yellowstone River flows right along the interstate.

> Mule train, (hyah, hyah!) clippity cloppin' over
> hill and plain.
> Seems as though they never stop, clippity clop,
> clippity clop clippity clippity, clippity, clippity,
> clippity clopping along!

That song, sung by Frankie Laine, I sang on the road to Miles City to keep players awake. Somehow, I thought it was appropriate. Somehow, the players didn't! Miles City is in the eastern side of Montana, where there are more cows than people—literally! It is the home to the internationally known "Bucking Horse Sale" in the third week of the month of May. It had become the largest horse market in the world. Needless to say, it is a classic cowboy town (which is not a putdown). Western boots are a big seller in town. We get off at the Haynes Boulevard Exit and are headed to the Red Rock Village on Valley View Boulevard. Shortly, Haynes makes an abrupt left to downtown, but the large sign says, "Straight ahead to Red Rock Village." It was an old dusty dirt road! My first thought was, *What the heck am I getting us into?* After a mile or so, Valley View shows up. Another big sign tells us to turn left.

Soon, there it is, Red Rock Village, a group of one-story rooms surrounding a two-story office, with a dinner club above it. We checked in. One night at the Red Rock, the owners invited our team up to the dinner club for an old-fashioned buffalo steak dinner. I had never eaten buffalo, but discovered it was very good. Also, nutritionists will tell you that it is better for you than beef steak, because it is leaner. Afterward I found a place that sold buffalo burgers. For the rest of my time in Miles City, if I had a burger, it was a buffalo burger.

Anytime a team arrives at a new or different town, the first thing the players want to do is scout out the ballpark. Denton Field was a 1940s' ballpark, but kept up fairly nicely. It had a covered grandstand with bleachers on both sides of the infield. The field had interesting dimensions: 312' down the left field line with a short three-foot fence, 321' down the right field line with a six-foot fence, and 438' to dead center. We called it "Death Valley!" However, it looked like a fun place to play.

The Cards had a so-so tournament in Miles City, losing to Rapid City and Scottsbluff, Nebraska, and defeating Grand Junction and Colorado Springs. We had fun, though. The stands were always full, and it seems the fans really took a liking to the Claremont Cardinals, always rooting for us. In Miles City, we had more than baseball teams to battle—mosquitoes! On top of that, we had a gold uniform and gold sanitary socks. That color seemed to attract those little critters. The stores were running low on skeeter spray! Early in the morning, you would see city trucks spraying for them. We fought off baseball teams and mosquitoes all week, but survived in the end. We then headed to Laramie Tournament, where we swept to win the tourney for the second time. I had the idea of putting on our newly created "phantom infield" before a game, so I asked the opposing coach if he would mind if we did so. He said no, he didn't want to see "any fool-ishness!" So we put that idea to bed for another time and went on to win the tournament. It was at the motel in Laramie that our players, myself included, learned the game of Pac-Man.

When we got home, we still had ten conference games to play. The Cards were 8–2 in those games, and that got us into District Playoffs, which we hosted at Claremont McKenna College. We opened with a 15–5 victory over Walnut, lost a tough 6–5 game to El Monte, defeated Arcadia 7–6 in ten innings, taking us into the finals, where we had to beat El Monte twice. Our ace, Randy R., shuts them out in the first game, 4–0, and we prevail in twelve innings in the second game, 9–7. We played twenty-one innings that day in ninety-five-degree weather with one catcher. "Iron Mike" was forced to catch every inning because our other catcher, Adam W., was injured and could not play. After the games were over, "Iron Mike" looked like he'd been to war! He had! And was officially presented with a faux medal of honor.

We move on to Area Playoffs in Northridge. Big wins against Santa Monica and Ventura set us up to face Chatsworth for the title and the right to go to State. They had to win two games. We lose the first game, 8–3, but it's Big Mac's home runs that lead us to an 18–4 championship at Area. We are going to State!

The American Legion flies us from Ontario to Oakland for State Playoffs in Yountville. Unfortunately, one of our better players, Dave, had left town and was at a family affair on the other side of the country. I contacted him, and he flew to Oakland, where we got him a ride to join us for the playoffs. He missed the first game.

Yountville is a small town, about forty-five miles north of Oakland airport, noted for its Veterans Hospital, which has a beautiful baseball field on the grounds. We are assigned a military-type bay to house our players, right next to a team from Fullerton. We open up against a Northern California team, Lodi. Randy R. is on the hill again and throws another gem, defeating Lodi, 4–1. The stands are filled with veterans who live at the hospital. We looked very good, and these old veterans started betting money on us to win the championship.

After the Lodi game, the next game would be an early morning one against another northern team from Albany, near San Francisco. That evening, I was hoping that our players could get a good night's rest before we had to play the early morning game. We had a problem, though. The Fullerton team didn't play until later in the day, so they were partying it up right next to us. They had a radio blaring music, were drinking and shouting back and forth. Finally tired of it all, Big Mac, a bruiser, got up, walked into their bay, snapped the radio off, and said, "Good night, gentlemen!" That was that, we didn't hear another peep from them.

We got up early and went to our game. Early in the game, an Albany player slid hard into second base to break up a double play. He doesn't go directly toward the bag but is looking for our shortstop to upset him. Randy, who pitched great yesterday, is our shortstop today and has his leg kicked out from him and tears up his knee. He has to go to the hospital and returns on crutches. In those days, the slide was legal because the runner could reach the base; consequently, nothing was done about it. Randy is out for the rest of the tournament. In a wild game, we lose, 17–14, and that holds over until the next day when we lose against El Segundo, 12–9. In that game, one of the weirdest play you will ever see occurred. With a runner on first for us, Crazy Danny hits a rocket off the left field fence. The left fielder chases it down, throws to the shortstop, who relays a strike to the catcher to nail our runner, trying to score from first. Danny, who is not our fastest runner, is rounding first and heads to second while the catcher makes a tag at the plate, pops up, and rifles a strike to the second baseman, who tags Danny out sliding in. He has hit the ball off the wall into a double play! Don't blame third base, Coach Greg. On the score card, it will look like this: 7-6-2-4 dp! Danny gets credit for a single. Two losses and you're out of the tourney. Our players, especially Dave, were upset. We felt we were better. The old-timers lost their bets. Our season is over, but overall, it was a good year.

As the next season rolls into view, a road trip becomes an important part of our schedule, and Miles City becomes a tournament must. As it turns out, for the next sixteen years, I will schedule our Cardinal games around the Miles City tourney. We will enter the event nineteen years in a row.

BACK UP THE TRUCK

In 1982, we had lost several key players to eligibility, but we still felt we had a good ball club. The Cards did pick up some key players to fill the roster. Keith W. came to us from the high school in La Verne. He was a big cuss but could run like a deer. Sam K. joins us and will become a great asset on the mound. Michael P. comes over from our archrival and will be voted our team MVP at the end of the season. He will hit, and complete, five games for us on the mound.

Once again, I scheduled an early season tournament at Santa Maria. After three straight wins, we lost the final game. The bus was not a problem. We went home to take on our league schedule. Our schedule was designed for 18–24 conference and local games as well as a three-week road trip. I always felt the importance in competing in a conference of teams for a title and to be able to go on and play postseason games. To me, that is where a season excitement exists. The road trip was special and added a degree of Americanism to our program.

For the second year, the Ogden Tournament was on our schedule. One night, after our game, several players went to the movies. They saw *Poltergeist* at the Cinedome in Ogden. It was a scary movie, and many players had a hard time getting to sleep after that. Most of the remainder of the trip, they slept with the lights on. We added a tournament in Billings, Montana, and of course, Miles City. We swept the tournament in Ogden and on the way to Billings, on US 14 through Yellowstone National Park, had an overnight stop in Cody, Wyoming. The town of Cody got its name from Buffalo Bill Cody, a famous showtime cowboy. The Buffalo Bill Center of the West, with many cowboy museums, is a very interesting place to visit if you are anywhere near Cody or Yellowstone. We took the double-dip rather easily, but having a California team stop in Cody was a big deal. There was a lot of fanfare and excitement from the locals. The local newspaper sent a reporter to cover our game, and of course, as in all small towns, the game was on the radio. The field was in good shape, and it was a sunken field. Cars would park above the field, and you could watch the game sitting in your car. Before the game, a reporter came up to me to talk to me about our team. We talked briefly. He took a few notes and then he asked, "What's the best thing you like about Cody?"

My quick response stopped him for a moment. "The water!" It was an honest answer. I don't know where Cody gets its water, but I thought that it was pure and delicious. Probably from the Shoshone River. The next morning, I read my answer in the local sports section of the *Cody Enterprise*.

On our tour of Yellowstone, we stopped by the side of the road to watch a herd of buffalo. Both Greg and Jeff thought it would be a good idea to touch one of them. I warned them not to, but that didn't stop them. The buffalo lowered his head, pawed some dirt, and busted after them! Luckily, there was a tree nearby that they used to put some space between them and the beast. Greg relates that he could hear it snorting and could smell its breath. He took a picture of it with his Kodak Instamatic Camera. The rest of the team watched in amazement. They thought it was the funniest thing they've seen! Nobody knew how dangerous it could have been.

When leaving Yellowstone, we passed the Madison River. The Madison runs north out of Yellowstone and flows into the Missouri

River. I pulled the bus over at a clear spot and told the players to change into their gold unis. We lined up along the river and took our first team picture on the road. Back on the bus, we changed out of the uniform. We have taken a team picture somewhere on the road every year since. You can see most of them in the picture section of this book.

Onward to Billings. Our reception by the Little Leaguers was almost as big as it was earlier. They were there and again wanted autographs, even during the game. Michael P., a rookie, led off for us in our first game. He weakly popped out to second. On the way back to the dugout, a young kid stuck out a ball and pen over the rail and asked for an autograph! Michael had never given an autograph, so he proudly signed the ball for the kid. I saw this and glared at him with disgust and a smirk. When he got back to the dugout, someone shouted, "Well, look at that, boys, Michael's popping out and signing autographs!"

West Covina was in the Billings Tournament, and they were accused of stacking their team with illegal players. I was asked to confirm or deny the accusation, since we were in their league. They were, and were booted from the tourney. This upset them, so they left their motel without paying. It was also where we stayed, and a story evolved and got back to American Legion headquarters that a California team skipped out on their hotel bill. Naturally, we were blamed because we were the "only" team that traveled like we did. It took a while to convince the powers that be that it was not us! Developing good relationships would be very important for us to continue each year on the road. Next stop, Miles City.

We played well in the tournament. We won five straight games before dropping the championship game, 4–1, to Yakima, Washington. Sam pitched a good game for us, but we were up against a future major league pitcher named Maddux. On our way home from Miles City, some players indicated that they were not feeling well. I don't know what it was, but we made a stop in Big Timber, Montana, and made a decision that any player who wanted to fly home, could. They would have to pay their way. I was surprised when most of the team volunteered to fly home, so after making several calls to California, making reservations on some airlines, and an overnight stay in Big Timber, we all piled into the bus and drove seventy-five miles back to the closest airport, Billings. Those who made reservations were allowed to leave and make their connections. We will see you next week. We have nine league games to go. The rest of us, not many, would finish the trip on six wheels! In the beginning, this bothered me, but I soon got over it, realizing that maybe this was the way to go. Upon returning home from a successful trip, I thought it was time to ditch our bus. Overall, it served its purpose, but we needed to move on. I sold it in October to "Campesinos Unidos de Brawley," farm workers of Brawley, a town near the Mexican border.

NEW WHEELS

I n May, as the high school season was winding down, since I was
head baseball coach at Claremont High School, it became time to
determine the roster for the summer team. The 1983 season will
become the year of the largest turnover of players in the twenty years,
filling the roster with fifteen new faces. The Legion team was com-
prised of players from three different high schools, and it wasn't dif-
ficult to recruit players. Actually, they probably recruited themselves.
A Catholic school in our league had become an archrival, but several
of their players contacted me about playing. Eventually, we picked
up five players from that school. One was their top player, Scott M.
My number one player, Daren H., expressly informed me that, "If he
plays, I'm not playing!"

My response was, "Well then, you'd better find a place to play
this summer because he will be on the team!"

Soon, Daren backed down, and it didn't take long for them to
develop respect for each other and become team leaders. I also had
to iron out travel arrangements for the summer. Fortunately, at our
school, one of our new young player's father owned a towing company in Pomona, a town adjacent to Claremont. Since Paul S., the
son, would be going on the road with us, the father would provide us

with another bus—this time, a 1965 long-nosed Ford school bus. This year, the bus would have to take us to Santa Maria, Lethbridge, Great Falls, and Miles City. Got a little driving to do!

Early in the 1983 season, we had a double-dip scheduled in Anaheim about thirty miles away. I had just picked up our latest bus and thought it would be a good time to give it a trial run. The team met at the high school and boarded the bus for the short run to Anaheim. We took the 57 freeway, an eight-lane highway, toward the beach. While driving down the freeway, a player comes up behind me in the driver's seat and says, "Coach, what's that smell?"

"I don't know, but I smell it. Smells like oil burning."

Just then, *ka-thunk!* The left front wheel comes flying off the bus. Holy cow! I've driven two buses, and on both, a wheel has come off. It was the left front wheel, and again a tire company had not tightened the wheel enough. I knew that I would have to steer to the fast lane and onto the side of the freeway, in the middle. I checked the rearview mirror and saw that the cars following me had slowed or moved to another lane, so it was safe. Thank goodness the wheel didn't bounce over the divider into oncoming traffic. Several parents driving to the game pulled over behind us, and I told the players to exit through the emergency back door. If they exited out the side door, they'd be stepping into the fast lane. We piled into the parents' cars and went to the game. Paul S. called his father, who sent out a tow truck to take the bus back to the yard.

We won the two games, 8–2 and 4–3, and headed back home. We are supposed to leave on the trip in two weeks, and I'm now concerned as to how we are going to go. Following the Anaheim doubleheader, we once again were entered into the Santa Maria Tournament. This time, we drove our own cars, while the bus stayed home for repairs.

How to gain a nickname that sticks is the story here. Donny N., a big, tall right-hander, was in a car that pulled into a drive-through. He wasn't feeling well and promptly threw up, or as they say, "Blew chips." He forever was called Chips! He spent two years on the Cardinals and won ten games.

After a 7–3 win over Norwalk for the tournament championship, we came home to good news. The bus would be ready. This was great news, although I didn't feel secure. On the day before we left, our ace pitcher, Nick C., threw a complete game, nine innings, to beat a very good conference rival, West Covina, 2–1 at home. This gave us a very positive send-off. On the way north, we stop in Las Vegas at a casino and take our next team picture. I wanted team pictures from different places, and a pause in Vegas provided us with the opportunity to get a picture there, as well a short rest.

The road to Canada is I-15, which goes all the way to a port called Sweetgrass. We leave Great Falls after lunch there, and eighteen miles south of the Canadian border, as I'm driving along, all of a sudden a small missile hits my windshield from inside. It was a piece of ice. I holler back, "Stop throwing ice! You are distracting the driver."

If you've ever ridden a bus, and I'm sure most people have at one time, you should note that the driver has a large inside rearview mirror where he can see every passenger. So I'm keeping my eye on the road and the mirror. In a few minutes, I spot John C. tossing some ice at a player seated right behind me. His aim was not too good, and it hit me on the shoulder. I became a little upset and pulled the bus over to the side of the road and stopped. "John, get your gear and get out of the bus!" He had a dazed look on his face and seemed somewhat bewildered. I repeated myself. John brought his gear to the front of the bus, wondering what I was going to do. I let him stew a little bit, then pointed to a green road sign about a mile up the road, "See that sign? Get off the bus and I will pick you up there!" John had to hoof it about a mile, carrying his gear with him as we waited for him at the sign. At first, the other players were quite amazed, but soon they made fun of it, and several took pictures of John carrying his luggage on the road. I felt that having to hike a mile with all your gear would have a bigger impact than a $10 per diem fine. I had no more problems with anything being thrown on the bus afterward.

When you cross the border into Canada, you definitely feel like you are in a different world. Gas is by the liter, every sign is in French and English, and there are no dollar bills, just coins. The one-dollar coin is a loonie, and the two-dollar coin is a twoonie. The one dollar gets its name from the loon, a bird, on the flip side. The two-dollar bill gets its name from the fact that it's two dollars! Distances are measured in kilometers, and you should learn the conversion rate. One kilometer equals roughly six-tenths of a mile. A hundred kilometers is 62 miles. At first, it gets confusing, but you get used to it. Another thing that must be done is go to the bank and cash in your US dollars for Canadian. To pay in Canadian is a lot easier for the cashier at whatever store. It also makes it easier for the players. There is a conversion rate for money, but it is flexible from day to day. I wanted my players to get their per diem in Canadian, which at the time meant $13 Canadian, to pay for things that way. They would be more comfortable doing so. As a point, if you save proof of sales tax you paid, you could stop at the border on the way back and get it refunded. We cross the border into Alberta. No guns, no alcohol, no tobacco, no problem. This was 1983, so a driver's license or birth certificate was fine, especially for the minors.

Lethbridge is about 65 miles north of the border in Alberta, or 105 kilometers. Henderson Field was right across the street from our motel, Super 8, so we were able to walk to the game. It was a beautiful ballpark with a large grandstands that circled home plate. It was a tough tournament except for our opening games with a team from Fort Saskatchewan, Alberta. Because we were in a bus, I thought it would be wise to have a car for coaches to get around in. I rented a very inexpensive (read cheap) car from "Junk Cars are Us." We used the car right away to drive to a local establishment for a coaches' meeting. All the coaches in the tournament were there. I got my first taste of Canadian beer, even though the bottle may have had an American label on it. It didn't take me long to realize that it had a much higher potency than the beer I once had while in the army at Fort Sill, Oklahoma (3.2), or even at home. I limited my intake to two beers.

One day we had an 8:00 a.m. game. I hate that! Anyway, I wanted the players to be awake for the game, so I got them up real early. The motel had a restaurant and bakery in it, and I had spoken to the baker at the restaurant the day before and made arrangements to have fresh cinnamon rolls ready for the players when they got up. To my surprise, they were large rolls, and with milk and juice, the players were fed a breakfast. The bakers went out of their way to make sure we had something good to eat. I gave them a very nice tip—Canadian, of course!

During the tournament, Daren H. had made friends with the young son of a sportscaster in town. Actually the whole team did. We gave him one of our caps, and that is all he wore on his head. Later in the year, after we had gotten home, his father sent me a nice letter and some gear from Lethbridge. Lethbridge also guaranteed us $1,000 loonies to come to the tournament. In our game with them, I got into a small argument with the umpire, holding up the game. Some fans became irritated and hollered, "Go back to California!" We hadn't been paid yet, so I yelled back, "I would, but you owe us a thousand loonies!" Of course, that kind of started something. You tell your players to keep their head out of the stands and then give them a bad example. Overall, our first experience in Canada was a good one, despite a battle with rain. I know we will be back.

We head back to Sweetgrass and the US border. We had no problem getting back into the country, no contraband to declare. Rolling down the I-15 once again, headed to Great Falls, about twenty miles north of the city, the engine starts to get hot and steam up. Geez, what now? We pull over to the side of the road and lift the hood. The designated mechanic isn't quite sure what the problem is. We let the bus cool down, push it off of the interstate at the Vaughn exit. The players started to play a football game. There was very little traffic, so the Claremont Cardinals played football in the middle of the I-15 interstate—true. While the football game was continuing, a van, with a family, was approaching, so the players moved out of the way, but the van pulled over, and the driver got out and asked, "What's the problem?"

I told him that I wasn't sure, so he grabs some tools out of his van and climbs into the engine and tinkers around. He says that we need a water pump. Where are we going to get one of those? No problem, he has a friend with an old Mercury in his backyard, and we can go get it and put it in our bus. Ford makes Mercury, so it should be a fit.

I mention to him that we have reservations at a hotel in Great Falls, and he volunteers to make room for several of our players and take them into the city. He then took his family home, drove back to the bus, and picked up the rest of the players. He and I then went to his friend's house and removed the water pump from the Mercury. It cost me $25. We drove back the eighteen miles, where we began the surgery on the bus. By this time, it was about 1:00 a.m. The first thing we would need is a gasket. We had none, so I grabbed a thick piece of cardboard and carved one out. He jumps into the engine and begins to take out the old water pump. I hold a small flash light while he replaces the pump. Done, start up the engine. All is good. I ask him how much he wants for all his troubles. While we are working on the bus, conversation led to the fact that I was from Southern California, and citrus country at that, so he says all he wants for his troubles is a crate of oranges for his family. He gave me his address, and I sent him a crate of oranges at Christmastime.

We split with the two Great Falls teams, the Electrics and the Chargers, losing the last game of the tournament, which became the beginning of a four-game skid entering the Miles City tournament. At the time, GF was a minor league affiliate of the Dodgers, so the ballpark was in good condition.

As you can imagine, Miles City was a down year for us. Actually 1983 was our worst showing in the tournament. We did finish on a high note when our ace, Nick C., threw a 10–0 shutout against Casper, Wyoming, to finish the trip. This is not necessarily a statistic story, but it is interesting that Nick gave us a good send-off with a big conference complete win and then gave us a big needed victory to end the trip. Nick pitched some great games for us that season. He was 9–4, with 104 Ks in ninety innings that year. Keith W. will be our MVP, hitting .440 with 45 runs scored and 55 RBIs. In two seasons, Keith had stolen fifty-nine bases and been thrown out only four times.

Moving on! The following year will become the last year that the Claremont Cardinals will travel by bus. Dominic M. an intense, exciting player will join the Cardinal roster and become an integral player on the Cardinals for two seasons. The year 1984 will see the schedule include five tournaments—three local, including our own "Cardinal Classic." The road will include a tournament in Billings and the Miles City Newhouse. We will also visit the Grand Tetons, where we will take our annual team picture. Yellowstone, once again, is on our schedule.

The Cardinal Classic is something new for us. I just decided, we travel to other teams' tournaments, so why not have one at home? It was a five-team affair with local Southern California teams, including Pomona, Redlands, Anaheim, La Habra, and ourselves, a good mix of teams. We split our four games.

After the weekend tournament, we had a few days off and began our conference schedule with Pomona at their place. About the seventh inning, our skinny young second baseman, David K., was at the plate against a hard thrower. We are in the first base dugout. David swings at a fastball and fouls it off. I'm standing on the first base side of the dugout and thinking, *Where is the ball?* It didn't take long to get an answer—it hit me square in the left eye! My glasses were shattered, and I thought glass might have gotten into my eye. As I fell to the ground, I kept telling myself to be quiet and that the worst was over. They hauled me off in an ambulance. I was in the hospital for four days. Consequently, I missed the Camarillo Tournament that weekend. It was reported to me that we lost two out of three. I returned for the Fullerton tournament, where we had the same results.

On our way to Billings, we slipped in a victory over Las Vegas on a hundred-degree-plus evening. In the morning, we headed up I-15 once again, until it met I-80 near Salt Lake City, east on I-80 to Evanston, Wyoming, and making a left on US 189 north, through Kemmerer, Wyoming, the home of Penney's Department Store. La Barge, Big Piney, and Pinedale are the small towns we zip through until we reach US 191. The road US 191 also took us through Jackson Hole, Wyoming, and the Grand Tetons, where we took the ski lift to the "top of the world." What a ride on the swinging gondola to the top of Snow King Mountain. The Cards won the championship of the Billings tournament, although lost a tough one-run game to Rapid City, a new nemesis. A pit stop in Sheridan, Wyoming, for a doubleheader garnered two more wins for us. The game highlight of the year, however, was a 5–3 victory over defending national champions, Belleview, Washington, in the Miles City tournament. Big John D. was locked in a tough 2–2 game before the Cards exploded for three runs in the seventh. Big D singled home the go-ahead run after a two-run home run by cousin Big Paul tied it up. Cuz had also doubled in the first for an RBI. Cousin Paul K., from Laramie, Wyoming, had enrolled at Claremont High School in 1983, in the second semester of his senior year, just to play high school baseball. Because his high school in Laramie didn't have a baseball program, the California Interscholastic Federation okay-ed him to play at Claremont. He brought along with him brother Pete. They played two years for Claremont High School and the summertime Cardinals.

We lost the semifinal game to Las Vegas Valley. While in Miles City, Eddie F., who I found out was a ladies' man, had made friendships with a certain cutie at the ballpark who came by the motel to visit him. I made sure that the visit was not in his room, but they could be outside. Eddie and his friend were lying down on the grass, with no blanket, and basically talking for a while. When Eddie got up, he was covered with welts and bug bites. Have I mentioned mosquitoes in Miles City? I actually felt bad for him. Eventually he recovered after some razzing from his teammates. We left Miles and headed home.

The Cardinals leave Miles City headed west, picking up I-90 past Billings, about 145 miles. Nearly 200 miles down the road from Billings is a small town called Whitehall, where I plan to exit and take a shortcut south to Dillon, Montana. We also need a break, so I pull over at a truck stop right off the freeway. Several players need a restroom, but it is crowded, and a few players decide to go around to the side of a semitrailer and do their thing. What they didn't know was that it was below a hilltop where there were houses. A little girl was playing in her backyard and spots the players relieving themselves down below. The girl tells her mother. She calls the police. By this time, I had reloaded the bus and we left for the cutoff.

Two blocks down the road, I pull over again at a less busy pit stop, and players were buying food for the ride. Just then, a man in civilian clothes approaches me with a gun on his hip and a badge on his chest. He is the local cop, the only one. He says he has a report of players exposing themselves back at the truck stop, and the mother wants to press charges. Egad! If that happens, we would have to stay around overnight and appear in court in Butte in the morning. Is there another solution? The plainclothes officer says if the players would go back with him and face the lady and apologize, she would not file charges. We get together with the team and explain the alternatives, and two players fess up. They go with the officer and make the sincere apology. We are back on the road for home. We leave Whitehall, find Montana 41 highway, and take it to Dillon, where it meets I-15.

COME FLY WITH ME

That's right, the Cardinals are going to fly to their original destination and then rent vehicles to take them around. We will leave Ontario Airport at 6:15 a.m. and fly to Minneapolis, Minnesota. There, we will pick up the vans, check into our motel, and drive to the Humphrey Dome, where we will watch the Twins play. The dome is basically a large balloon filled with air! The roof is an off-gray, which makes it hard to follow the ball. When you walk in, it sucks you in. When you walk out, it blows you out. We have good seats for a group, as the players are in four rows at third base. Midway through the game, I get the belief that a couple older players are having a beer. What? How'd you get those? Come to find out, the youngest player on the team, Sean B., had bought them for Dave H. and another. Sean looks twenty-three but is actually fifteen, and wasn't even carded. Nobody hurt, but $10 per diem fine all around.

The next morning, I get a message that one of our rooms was very loud over the night. Players were excited about flying and seeing the major league game at the dome, so they apparently hadn't settled down. When I went into the office to pay the bill, I received a stern rebuke. I had to admonish all our players, "We are in a motel and there are other people here. Keep that in mind, while we are on the road."

Claremont is headed northwest up I-94 to Moorhead, Minnesota, for a tournament in two cities: Moorhead and Fargo, North Dakota. They share the border created by the Red River, a rare river that runs north, out of the country, into Manitoba, Canada, and flows into lower Lake Winnipeg. We turn in our rental vans for two vans from the local Christian college, thanks to the head coach, Bucky. The Cards check into a motel right on the river. What a difference in culture the river separates. Fargo is ranching and farming with prime black soil, while Moorhead is very primp and stodgy. It's close to the Fourth of July, so several players want some fireworks. They are illegal in Minnesota, but all you have to do is walk across the bridge into Fargo and you can find them on any corner. This could become a problem. It did!

During the night, I hear some bottle rockets go off outside. Was that on our side of the river or the other side? I don't know. A short time later, more fireworks. I'm not particularly bothered by it, but should have been. About three in the morning, I hear a loud knock on my door. It's the Moorhead police! Now I'm particularly bothered! Several of the players were lighting off fireworks, and it's illegal. We got a stern warning about it, and the players got a lecture from me— albeit, my heart was not in it. This was our introduction to Minnesota, and the local folk were not impressed.

College head coach Bucky was also their legion coach. He had heard about our episode with the fireworks and the police. The vans were gratis, but coach threatened to take them away. Our relationship with Moorhead is off to a rocky start. Coach Jerry and I started looking around to see if we could find alternative transportation in case Bucky decided to follow through with the threat. We could take a bus or a train. He softened up after his team defeated us, 3–1, in the tourney. On the other side of the river, where most of the games were played, relations were much better. We finish the tournament and are declared tied with Moorhead for the title. Next stop, Billings. Bucky has decided to allow us to continue our journey in the college vans. That saved us a lot of money.

On the road, the players are responsible for washing their own personal clothes, but the coaches will wash their uniforms. After a game, just pile them up in front of the coaches' room and they will be taken care of. That responsibility was placed on Coach Jerry, who had a system to get the unis washed quickly at a Laundromat. He gained the nickname from the players as "Zippy the Laundryman." That carried over to the van he drove, Zippy's van.

On our way to Billings, we make a sightseeing stop at Mount Rushmore in South Dakota. This was a first for almost all our players. I thought it would be a great place for our next team picture, so the players brought their unis from the vans and we suited up. I asked a few visitors if they would allow us to get the team together for the picture. No problem.

We cruise into Billings with far less fanfare than in the past. We were a second place team in Billings with a win over their Scarlets and a loss to the Royals. In the Royals game, I hollered to one of our players on the bench to "grab a bat." He got excited thinking he was going to hit. That isn't what I had in mind—"Kill that spider!"

We scored thirty-seven runs and allowed four to a team from Blackfoot, Idaho, including a 24–4 whitewash, but it wasn't enough to capture the tourney championship. We stayed at a motel in the Heights. It was a nice enough motel, but Billings was suffering from a grasshopper infestation. The motel outdoor pool was full of grasshoppers, and no one wanted to go swimming in it. It was also a little isolated, so players became antsy. It was tough to get them down at night with all-night action going on. We survived.

We headed south to Thorne-Rider Stadium in Sheridan, Wyoming, and stayed at the Holiday Inn there. We had a good showing in Sheridan, winning the championship. You could hear it on KWYO, Sheridan. During our stay, there became an interesting development on the team. While we are on the road, only a few players would show up for breakfast, usually the same few. Coach Jerry and I were always there, also. The players decided to start a "breakfast club" on the team, and they included the coaches. Xavier A., was elected president. Nothing like starting a clique, but in some ways that is what it was. I admit, I carried it forward by having T-shirts made, signifying the Claremont Cardinals Breakfast Club. Afterward, a few other players began to join us, but the only time the entire team was required to come to a breakfast was if we had an early morning game. Of course, an incentive was to get your $10 daily per diem early.

Miles City was next on our road schedule. We have moved out of the Red Rock Village and into the Buckboard Inn, right next to McDonald's. Actually, the Buckboard is in a very good location for us. Besides McDonald's, there is a restaurant a block away and also a grocery store two blocks away with a good deli, open all night, and the Buckboard had an outdoor swimming pool. When I was looking for motels in Miles City, that was a prerequisite for me, an outdoor pool. All the other motels had pools, but they were all indoors, so the Buckboard was it. We were hot and cold again in Miles City and wound up in second place, losing a semifinal game to our friends from Las Vegas. Coach Bucky of Moorhead, whose team was also in the tournament, wanted to take his vans home from Miles City, which was not a bad idea, since I didn't want to drive them back to Minnesota. We hired a bus to pick us up at our motel and rode it back to Billings, where we boarded our plane to go home.

When I was recruiting for our summer team, I looked for some players from our archrival school. We had played them in the high school league at their place, and our game was over early, but we were traveling with the freshmen and they were still playing, so I sat on the bus keeping watch on the freshmen. However, I spotted two varsity players from our rivals who were still hitting in a cage, getting in extra work. I took note of that and decided I would like them to play in the summer. Later, in the high school season, I went to one of their practices and asked their coach if I could talk to them. Xavier A. and Tim M. seemed very interested and excited that I was talking to them. They signed up and became a very big part of our season.

After the road trip, we split six conference games and went into the District Playoffs. We couldn't solve West Covina losing to them six times, including twice in district. Overall, on the season, West Covina outscored us, 76–26. Ouch!

Turning the page, I start planning for the year 1986. We added some key players to our roster from another local high school, including a future major league player, Kevin F., who was one of the fastest players I've ever had. Another exciting player, Junior P., came from our rival school. Junior was a hard-nosed little guy who got on everyone's nerves, especially if he was on the other side. When we played them in the high school season, our guys hated him. When he joined the summer team, our guys loved him. You wanted him on your side—he was a winner.

Locally, Ontario had an early season tournament, and it was close by, so we opened with that. We swept through it and won the tournament. Before we hit the road, we had a twelve-game conference winning streak, so we were feeling good when we took off from Ontario and headed to the first of three tournaments: Lethbridge, Billings, and Miles City.

I made time for us to travel through Yellowstone once more, where we take our team picture at Tower Falls. The falls are behind us with a huge boulder above them. I find out later that the boulder will come crashing down the following week. Also, while in Yellowstone, I have made reservations for a river raft trip down the Snake River. The Snake River is one of America's premier rivers, flowing 1,100 miles west from Yellowstone to the Columbia River in Washington State. It has a white water rafting rating of 3 to 4, depending on the time of the year or the water level, so it can be an exciting rafting trip with several large rapids. It was a guided trip, so I felt it would be safe because several of the players had never been on a rafting outing. What's more, a few players were thrown off the raft into the cauldron of water, including myself, which was a scary thrill in itself. Our team took two rafts for the trip, which meant that in still water we would have battles between the rafts. It was a great raft excursion. Still water runs deep!

We make it to Lethbridge and have our first encounter with a team from Taiwan, China. We played a tough game with them but lose, 3–1, and wind up in third place. Even with a loss, the players felt good that they had played toe to toe with Taiwan. In Lethbridge, our motel is right across the street from the ballpark, so we would just gather all together and go to the field. I didn't take a head count.

For our Sunday game, I had posted the lineup, but we were missing a player during batting practice. Where is Timmy? His teammates dutifully kept quiet about it, protecting their teammate as best as they could, but after scratching Tim from the lineup, I was able to find out why he was missing. He went to church with a girl friend he met, and her family, and afterward, they went on a picnic. His explanation was that he lost track of time and that he wasn't aware it was as late as it was. I had several feelings about this whole story. Going to church and on a picnic is innocent, and I liked the idea of meeting local folks. Not being aware of the time is his fault, because all the players knew what the pregame routine was and the time of the game. His number one responsibility is to the team. Tim was one of our leaders, so I met with him to discuss this situation. He was remorseful about the second point. He did not play that game.

Back into the States, we are headed to Billings. We sweep Billings, part of an eight-game road trip winning streak. During one of the games, Doug T. is at the plate and begins a streak of eight straight foul balls as part of a twelve pitch at bat. After the tenth pitch, a foul ball, Daryl G. hollers from the bench, "*The Longest Day!*" in reference to the World War II movie. Doug was up there a long time. We are still signing autographs, but the Billings crowd is getting used to seeing the Claremont Cardinals in town.

The tournament in Miles City brings more excitement for the Cards. However, we will fall short of winning the title. The highlight of the tournament was the game against the always tough Yakima, Washington. The Beetles had built up a 4–2 lead going into the last inning. That's when the Cardinal bats come alive with a six-run rally, featuring a bases loaded two out single by Tim to tie the game, followed by a walk to Junior to reload the bases. Yakima changes pitchers, and Doug hits the new pitcher's first pitch for a grand slam home run. Six runs for the Cards turns the game around as Junior shuts down the Beetles in the bottom of the inning. This exciting finish made the Cards look like the team to beat in the tournament. We were beaten, though, by the home town Mavericks, 4–2, and nemesis Las Vegas Valley, 4–0. For the season, Tim was a middle infielder and had an amazing 104 putouts and 108 assists and participated in 33 double plays. These were all new high marks for our team.

OH! CANADA

The headlines read, "Another Late Show for Claremont" and "Miraculous Ending Is Par for the Course." Those two headlines in various newspapers marked our 1987 season. It started at the Fullerton Tournament with a ten-run last inning, after two outs, to beat a good team from La Habra, 10–8. It ended in the Miles City Tournament with a seven-run last inning over Rapid City, 9–8. The game was the last game of the night, and it had been delayed because of rain. It didn't start until around 11:00 p.m. Rapid City had built up a 7–2 lead after six innings with just twenty seconds to go in the time-limited game. We will play the seventh inning. An error, fielder's choice, four consecutive hits including Bill's bases loaded triple set the stage for Nick. Bingo, first pitch and it's two more runs! Another late night victory for the Cardinals. By the time the game was over, it was past 1:00 a.m. Miles City does everything they can to get the games in—I'll discuss that later in another chapter.

We head to the Buckboard, but our guys are still pumped over the win. How are you going to keep them quiet? These were my instructions: "Be quiet because we have neighbors. You have a 3:59 a.m. curfew [4:00 a.m. sounded too late!]. Go to the all-night restaurant, go to the deli at the all-night grocery store. Our next game will be at 8:00 p.m." The players handled it well.

The next day in the local newspaper, the *Miles City Star*, the headlines read, "Greatest Comeback in Tournament History." Earlier in the tournament, Glen C. picked up a tough win over Billings Royals, 3–2, on a squeeze bunt by Johnny in the top of the seventh. Junior finished the game with two strikeouts in the seventh for the save. Before we hit the road, we had an opportunity to play a team from Australia at home. Sean B., who has gained the nickname Boss, and Erik G. were given the task to pitch, but a six-run inning in the second put us too far in the hole, and we succumbed, 8–6. This is Boss's third year, and he will play one more. We started the road trip with twenty-one runs in Helena and head to Great Falls for two, which we split.

On I-15 once again headed to Lethbridge. We won five out of six in Lethbridge, but a tough 6–4 loss to another Taiwan team cost us the championship. It's Canada Day, like our Fourth of July, so we have our own picnic and watch their fireworks. Lethbridge is becoming a magnate with the Canadian ladies. One night, I get a call from the front desk. Have I seen someone's daughter? No? Well, Mom is on the phone and says her daughter is with a Claremont player. She lives 30 miles away in Taber (read 48 kilometers!). I go knocking on doors and come to Boss's room.

"Is anyone else in here?"

"No, we're trying to go to sleep."

I walk around the room and notice that the bathroom door is shut. Everybody in the room is accounted for, so why is the bathroom door shut? I knock on the door, and a squeaky voice comes back. I open the door and there is the Taber Lady!

"Call your mom and head home."

On this trip, after Lethbridge, we will be going north. On our way to Calgary, we headed north on Alberta 2, through Fort McCleod, and passed Buffalo Jump. A buffalo jump is a sharp cliff where stampeding buffalo simply charge off the cliff to their death. This is sixteen miles north of Stand Off, a village that serves as the headquarters of the Blood Indian Tribe of the Kainai Nation. Historically, they were responsible for causing the stampede of buffalo. We will visit Banff National Park, Lake Louise, and the Calgary Stampede, which is a rodeo and fair put together. But first we have exhibition game against a Calgary all-star team.

In a shortened ten-run rule game, Erik G. and Glen C. pitched well for a 17–2 win. Jorge was fined $2 for mentioning his high school. Because the Cards generally had players from three different high schools, I had a standing rule that if you mentioned your school, you would be fined. All monies went into the team coffers. Our first excursion away from Calgary is a trip to Banff and Lake Louise. It is 96 miles to Banff, or as they say in Canada, 155 kilometers. The trip is worth it. (See Lake Louise in the picture section.) The road to Banff, Trans-Canada Hwy-1, is mountainous and has its own beauty, especially a mountain range called the Three Sisters. The trip to Banff is an all-day adventure, so after returning to Calgary, we will go to a nice dinner. It was a great day all around.

Before we left on our trip, I had purchased tickets to the World's Largest Rodeo and Exhibition, so that is what is on the schedule for the weekend. Our motel, Relax Inn, is on the outskirts of the city, so we are going to take the train to the Stampede. The Calgary Stampede is a mixture of several adventures. It is a large rodeo that draws competitors from all over the world, horse races, including the exciting chuck wagon races, and it is a huge fair with exhibits and rides. There is something for everyone, but we have tickets to the rodeo, and I know that most of our Southern California boys have not attended one of those.

On the second day, we will go to the chuck wagon races, which was an experience in itself and a lot of fun. Most of the players also went to the fair, since we had plenty of time for that. That Saturday was the Fourth of July, so I felt we needed to show some American spirit and have a traditional picnic, in Canada. I had purchased watermelon and hot dogs and the fixin's and had found a park to go to. Didn't happen! It poured. Our picnic was inside a room at the motel with pizza!

The side trip to Calgary was an exciting way to get away from the baseball field for a couple of days. Leaving Calgary, we were headed to the Sheraton Inn in Great Falls for a stay, then on to Miles City. We lost a semifinal game to Bismarck, North Dakota, to end the tournament. A flight home follows a win over Sheridan, Wyoming. We have five conference games to go. The district playoffs were a bust as we lost both games that we played.

STATE CHAMPS '88

When we entered the 1988 season, the State Playoffs were on nobody's mind. We would have fifty games to play before any chance of that happening. Two things that I was sure of was (1) that our schedule was going to be trying and that (2) we had a good solid team. *Team* is the operative word here. We had no real big guns on the team, but we had lots of little guns. One of our smallest players, Lou D., led the team in home runs with seven.

After sixteen games, we had thirteen wins and were ready to hit the road. We take with us, on the trip, the scorekeeper, and a very bright individual, from Claremont McKenna College. Tony P. was a person I knew all the years I worked at the college, and he wanted to go to keep score for us. First stop after leaving Ontario and flying into Billings was a two-game set with Cody, Wyoming. Sort of a tune-up for the road. The opener was an awakening! To preserve our pitching, we started Coach "D," who we listed as "Others," and he claims a "perfecto" for seven hitters. The eighth hitter jacks one out of the park. After a couple more hitters reach base, the Cards are out of the inning on a play at the plate. The second time through wasn't any better. Once again, the number 8 hitter is at the plate with the bases loaded. He hits a grand slam to left field.

I go out to the mound, and I'm not happy. "How long do you want this to continue?"

To further debase the situation, you could hear the radio announcer describe Other's selection of pitches as, "not much of a fastball, not much of a curveball!" We lose the first game but roar back in the second with a 14–4 victory. Jorge P. led the charge in the second game with a two-run home run. We are moving on to Billings for a three-game series with the two Billings teams, the Royals and the Scarlets, in a two-day event. We split with the Royals and win the single game over the Scarlets. We "rolled a natural," allowing seven runs in each of the games but scoring eleven in the two wins.

Two games at Great Falls where Billy P., the repeller on the team, throws a complete game victory for a 6–2 win. Again, we can't get a sweep, falling short, 9–5. This is Billy's second season with us. We picked him up from a neighboring high school in '87, and he showed some prowess going 6–2 and hitting .352. In 1988, he went 11–3 and hit .368 with four home runs. On this little guns' team, Billy was a stalwart. Many people like to hike the mountains. On weekends, at home, Billy would repel those mountains.

From Great Falls, the Cardinals head north on I-15 until they reach US 2 at Shelby, Montana. There, they will make a left, drive to Browning, and pick up US 89, north. The Cards enter Glacier National Park at St. Mary's and travel the Going-to-the-Sun road to Logan Pass. They will stop along the way to take several pictures, including the team picture. Shots of Goose Island, on Lake St. Mary's, was also a popular scene. The gift shops at Logan Pass were popular, as players were able to purchase souvenirs of their time in Glacier Park.

Canada is calling, and we are answering the call. Lethbridge is next on our schedule. So far, our success on the road has not been good, and the players were starting to bicker among themselves. This is not good, and it was very irritating to me. We had beaten Taiwan 7–6, which I felt should help, but later we lost a game against Trail, British Columbia, and played poorly, so poorly, I got frustrated and left the game and went back to the motel, changed out of my uniform, put on a pair of swim trunks, jumped into the pool, and swam some laps to work it off. We had blown a sizable lead only to lose 15–14. When the players got back from the game, they saw me doing laps in the pool. Later, we got together in a team meeting to air out our grievances, and during the meeting, we discussed who should start the next game on the mound. Ernie R. had had two poor outings and was not happy with his performances. Suddenly, he spoke up and demanded, "I want the ball!" He got the ball and turned in a great performance and a win for the Cardinals.

From that moment on, the Claremont Cardinals won twenty-six games and lost four. To quote Johnny V., "We turned on a dime that very day in Lethbridge."

Lou D. was our second baseman, and he was a solid, aggressive ballplayer. I mentioned him earlier as our leading home run hitter. In our game with Taiwan, their second baseman had "Liu C." on the back of his uniform. He was on first, as a base runner, and tried to steal second. He was thrown out, tagged out by Lou D. The next day, in the *Lethbridge Herald*, there was a picture of the two, Lou D. and Liu C. Taiwan had stayed at the same motel as we had, so the two players got to see each other and developed a friendship. Lots of communication was with hand gestures, but it was a good friendship. To finish this story, when we got home, both Lou D. and Liu C. continued to communicate through letters to each other. I know Lou D. found someone to interpret his letters, and I'm sure Liu C. did the same. This is one of my all-time favorite stories about our travels. This is what baseball and sports are all about!

The evening before getaway day in Lethbridge, several players wanted to go downtown and get something to eat. I allowed them take a van. They climbed into a Suburban we had rented, with Johnny V., a player, driving. Sitting in the middle, up front, was Jorge P. As Johnny backed out of the motel parking place, he turned to go forward. At that moment, Jorge turned to answer a question from the back seat, and when he did, his left leg and foot kicked Johnny's right foot on the accelerator and the van lurched forward. They hit a small flatbed trailer, from Vermont, parked next to them. The players immediately jumped out of the van and scattered to their rooms. Coach Daren was with them, but was in the passenger seat up front. He knew that a player shouldn't be driving, so he went into one of the rooms and got a sweater from John to wear, to claim he was driving. I told the players to stay in their rooms. By this time, our neighbors, who owned the trailer, had become aware of what happened and called the constable. When he showed, he asked what happened. Coach told him that he was driving, and that is when the neighbors vehemently declared someone else was driving. After asking a few more questions and taking some notes, the constable said, "I don't care who was driving!" He wrote out his report. That was it! I was very relieved that we didn't have any charges made.

In the morning I told the players to stay in their rooms, while Coach Jerry found an auto body store and purchased the items we needed to fix the damage as best we could. Our front driver side fender had damage, and the left headlight was destroyed. We left for Miles City with the idea that we could not do any night driving.

When we arrived in Miles City, the Buckboard was again our way station. The first thing that had to be done was to find a place to repair the "attack Suburban." I found a repair shop, and they told me that it would take three days. Great, we will be in town longer than that, so we took it in. The last thing I wanted to do was to turn in a rental vehicle to Thrifty Car Rental in Billings with damage. I had made great relationships with them every time we flew into Billings. We spent the next several days shuttling the players from the motel to the ballpark and back.

When the van was ready, I paid the expenses out of the team found. One night, Jeff, Joe's brother, made a bet with some teammates that he could get a half a can of Skoal in his mouth. He did, and kept it there, and won $25. Keith P. came back to the motel one night with a hickey on his neck. Some of the players began to give him a little razzing, which made him somewhat angry. One player suggested that to get rid of it, put a frozen spoon on it. That did not go over with Keith.

We swept Miles City for our first championship of the tournament, scoring double-digit runs in every game, part of a seven-game streak of ten or more runs. The biggest game of that sweep came against California foe, El Segundo. The Eagles had built up an 8–2 lead through five innings. There remained twenty seconds left in the time limit game, so the Cards batted in the sixth and rallied for seven runs, led by Nick C.'s triple. They pick up two more in the seventh and go on to win a wild one, 11–10, vaulting them into the championship against Hancock, Michigan. Nick finished the game with three gutty relief innings. Ernie will finish the tournament on the mound, with a tournament championship two-hit shutout, 12–0, over Hancock. Afterward we made a quick stop once more in Sheridan, Wyoming, where we battled them for ten innings and a 11–8 end-of-trip victory. When we get home, we will have six more conference games to go before we open District Playoffs.

Playoff time is really a second season, a set of double elimination series where everyone starts 0–0. The Cardinals host District Playoffs at Claremont McKenna College, their home field. Arcadia provides the competition in the championship game, but the Cards win big, 13–3. Next is Area Playoffs. We open up with Camarillo in a wild 12–10 win. The plate umpire was an old nemesis of mine, and I managed to get thrown out of the game in about the seventh. Actually, I didn't deserve it. I had picked up a loose ball and made an underhand toss to him, intentionally short of him so it would fall at his feet. He got even with me. Our second game against Santa Monica doesn't go well, so it puts us in a hole. Finally, on a long hot Sunday afternoon in Pomona, we find ourselves playing Santa Monica again, and we have to win two! Boss gets the start on the hill and goes six innings, giving up six runs. Nick shuts the door the rest of the way while the offense is scoring eight runs to win. One game down! Ernie will start game 2, and he goes five innings, then Billy sandwiches himself in for two plus innings, to be closed out again by Nick, our very reliable closer. Jorge squeezes the catch on a fly ball to right to end this marathon, 11–8, and once again the Cards will board a plane in Ontario for Oakland.

Everyone has a ticket, but there are no names on the ticket, causing no problems at that time. Our stay in Yountville will be outside of the Veterans Administration in a motel in Vallejo. We learned to do this after our 1981 experience. I had to argue with the state chairman to convince him it would be all right, that we could handle it, since we have been on the road for twenty-one days and know how to handle ourselves. He gave in. We don't have to put up with another team's rowdiness this time. I preached to the team that going to state was not a vacation trip. "It's a business trip, and we are going to 'brown bag' it!" They understood.

The Cards are not 100 percent healthy headed to state. Lou has a broken index finger on his left hand, and Nick is recovering from a ten-inch gash in his hand, which will keep him out of the State Playoffs. Lou broke his finger taking a bad hop in the first game of the Area finals. He played both games that day by having it taped straight. It sticks out when he bats. Ernie will get the opener in state and goes all the way in a 7–1 victory. Johnny V. collects four hits, including two doubles to aid in the victory. Lafayette was our next opponent. At a pretournament players' meeting, one of my players heard a Lafayette player boast about how great their team was and how they expected to march right through the tournament. Our players took it to heart and made sure they would do something about it. The great part about it was, our players went about their business and quietly, without fanfare, ten-run-ruled them, 15–4. Boss went all the way on the mound, getting help from Lou's grand slam home run, on the first pitch to him in the fifth inning, with his broken finger pointing to left field. Lou's slam broke the game open and served to make the statement that the Cards had established themselves as the team to beat. We also were up 2–0 in the tournament, which earned us a day off.

It is always a problem as to what to do with your team off the field, and especially on a full day off. I learned that the Oakland As were in town. One of their players had played for the Claremont Cardinals, so I made contact with him through his father, who happened to be my dentist, to see if he could get us into the game. No problem. Mark

McGwire made arrangements for our team, a party of twenty-two, to have great seats at third base, and brought the entire team down on the field during batting practice, and took pictures with each one and the group. During the middle of the game, he also had a message on the big board introducing us as a team and wishing us the best of luck. I don't think we could have done any better on our day off.

Back to the business at hand, a game for the title against Merced. More action to come! Bill, who has developed into our ace starter, is rested for this one. The championship game, against Merced, gets a slow start, but by the end of the fifth, Merced leads the Cards, 6–4. Fireworks are about to start. In the bottom of the sixth, with a runner on base, Keith P. sticks his head out of the dugout with a bat and makes his first appearance in the tournament as a pinch hitter. On the first pitch he sees, Keith drives one over the left field fence to tie the game up. After he rounds the bases and returns to the dugout, I tell him that someone is going to go take his place on the field. Keith makes one appearance and sees one pitch in his state playoff career! In the seventh inning, Dustin L. is at the plate with a runner on, and after fouling off a couple pitches, he ties into a high fast ball and sends it over the same fence as Keith. The Cards take the lead, 8–6. Billy takes the mound in the eighth inning but gets into a little trouble, so with two runners on and one out, I bring in Carlos B. to finish this thing. He does, we win, and the pile-on is on! Sweet Potatoes! Dustin, our catcher, is selected as the Most Valuable Player. We are going to move on to Regional Playoffs in Albuquerque, New Mexico!

We board another plane in Ontario, and this time we head to Albuquerque with a change of planes in El Paso, Texas. Again, I have tickets for everyone with no names on them. We were allowed to take our team and two coaches, but we had an extra ticket, so I ask our third coach to use the ticket and join our entourage. Coach Charlie joins us and "up, up, up, and away we go!" The extra ticket is due to the fact that we have lost a key player, Lou. He must start classes at the University of Kansas, where he will play ball. Jeff F. will take his place at second base. Good news is, Nick is back in uniform and ready to play.

In game 1, we face Boulder, Colorado. We were stymied 7–1 in an 8:00 a.m. game. When you lose an 8:00 a.m. game early in a tourney, you are not going to get a better time to play in your next game. We will play four straight games at that time, so we will develop a new lifestyle. Once again, I remind the players that this is a business trip. Early to bed, early to rise, at six each morning. The night before, I will take orders from players and send Coach C. to McDonald's in the morning to pick up their orders and bring them back to our rooms. Batting practice at 7:00 a.m. is a must, if for no other reason but to shake the cobwebs out of their heads and wake them up. I'm not happy about it either!

Sean B. and Carlos B. take care of old friends Las Vegas Valley, 8–4, with Johnny V. leading the way offensively, with three RBIs. We have been playing at the University of New Mexico's Lobo Field, but in game 3 against Taylorsville, Utah, we move over to the triple "A" Albuquerque Dukes minor league field. At that time, the Dukes were a Dodger affiliate. Billy P. is on the bump, and he spins a nifty three hitter on 102 pitches in nine innings, 7–3. More sweet potatoes! Jorge and Mighty Joe I. lead this one at the plate, with everyone in the lineup getting a hit.

We are staying at the Ramada Inn in Albuquerque. Early on, I asked the concierge if there was a Mexican food restaurant nearby. Players had voted on what type of dinner they wanted. He told me there was a place about four blocks down the road, so that night, we gathered together and took a walk to the restaurant. It served not only Mexican food, but it was a New Mexican place. Take a lesson here, New Mexican food is spicier than Mexican food. I bought dinner for eighteen people, and only three could finish theirs. Too hot! I finished mine, one of the eighteen.

The Cards are bouncing back from the early loss, but they face Boulder again in game 4, and Ernie, who started against them in the first game, is the starting pitcher again. This time, he gets all the support he needs to go all the way for a 16–8 victory. Billy P. and Jorge P. hit back-to-back home runs in the seventh inning as both of them collect three hits and multiple RBIs. A huge victory and revenge for Ernie, but just as important, we get a later playing time! Boss, who is 10–0 on the season, gets the nod for this game, over Nick C., against hometown Albuquerque. Nick is not happy! Boss struggles this time, giving up six runs in the first two innings. Carlos and Nick finish the game, but it is the end of the season for us as we drop this fifth game, 12–3. What a great year!

When we get home, I get a call from a local newspaper, and one of the questions was about us being losers at regional playoffs. I informed him that we were State champs and that I certainly wouldn't call us losers. It was kind of irritating. Also, when I returned, I got a call from the State American Legion director concerning the "extra ticket." He claimed that we had not used it for a player and that we broke the rule about only two coaches. My argument was that I had never been to a regional and was unaware of these strict rules, believing we could use the tickets that were issued. After all, there were no names on them. Whether, he accepted my explanation or not, I don't know, except to say the case was dropped. The year 1988 was the Claremont Cardinal's finest year. As I mentioned in the beginning, we had no big boppers, just a bunch of little ones. We had chutzpah, a huge desire, and a never-quit attitude. The 1988 team accepted all challengers with a team feeling that we would win. It was so much fun to sit back and watch them work.

NORTH DAKOTA BOUND

There is no way we are going to match last season. The Cardinals will lose some key players but will fill those holes with new blood that will carry them forward for another couple of years. Bobby B., Randy D., Steve E., Jason H., Brian L., John M., Chris R., Paul R., Mike S., Bob S., Scott B., Brett C., and Jeff I., Joe's brother, will all help support the returning players. Jorge has one more year. Keith, who hit the key pinch home run in State, will be back. Ernie R., who was 8–2 last year, is an important returnee. That's about it. We will be a new club, but hopefully those who return can help show the way. One of the best finds, as a player and pitcher, was Bobby B. I had filled seventeen spots on the team and wanted one more and was looking for a pitcher. Bonita High School had one, but he had not been recruited. I called Bobby to see if he was interested in playing. He wasn't home. Where was he? Golfing, a very positive answer. I also learned he was a wrestler on the high school team, weighing in at something like the 109 lbs. He may have been small in stature, but he was tall in heart! Did I mention that he was a lefty? Wow! I want this guy! All my questions about him were being answered with very positive answers—he'll be a winner. Bobby wanted to play and was excited when I finally was able to contact him. With such a large turnover in players, it's going to be like starting all over. But we haven't stopped traveling. Another year, other destinations.

After a tournament championship, once again in Ontario early in the season, and a few conference games we will be headed north, and this year farther east. I like the Ontario Tournament because it gives us an early season chance at competition where we can evaluate exactly what we have, and this year, 1989, with a new squad, that will be important. What has developed in these games at home has been a very potent lineup. When the season is over, we will have had three players with over a .400 batting average, led by Jorge at .447, and two newbies, Chris R., and Jason H., who will be referred to as Brawny, from now on. Brawny got his nickname because he looks like the picture on the paper towel package, Brawny. Plus, he is a big boy! He cleans up a mess!

The Sheridan, Wyoming, Tournament is on the schedule, as well as our now annual trip to Miles City. Also, we will be headed farther east into Teddy Roosevelt country to Bismarck and Mandan, North Dakota. The parents in Bismarck will put on a large indoor barbecue for us, and in Mandan, the next day, we will visit Fort Lincoln, where General Custer was stationed before he left for Montana and the Battle of the Little Big Horn River. I love history, and I fully believe our youth should learn it.

We fly out of Ontario once again to Salt Lake City, where we will change planes for Billings, must be Delta. Thrifty Car Rental again, also. After leaving Billings going east, we pick up I-94 headed to Sheridan. Holiday Inn in Sheridan, with a waterfall in the middle of the hotel, is our temporary home. We sail through the tournament and win the championship. We have a date in Lethbridge. We make it there and check into our favorite Super 8. While we are in town, let's have a picnic, so we go down into the gorge for a Cardinal picnic along the Saskatchewan River. It was a nice day so in the spirit of team pictures, I decide we will take our team picture with the Lethbridge in the background. The bridge is the longest and highest railroad trestle in America, spanning the gorge and the river for over a mile.

The next day, in the middle of the game, one of my players reports to me, after being called out on strikes, that the umpire had told him, "Swing the f—— bat." I'm thinking, this is not what the umpire should do or say, just because he's covering up for a rotten call, so I go out there, and in my inimitable way proceed to tell him what I think about his call and language. He throws me out of the game, but in doing so, he knocks my glasses off and breaks the frames, unintentionally, of course. I have to tape up the glasses to be able to wear them and will go around the rest of the trip looking like a geek (no offense to geeks).

The next morning, Coach Daren H. and I go to the constable department to file a complaint. I was told that I had no case because I was not a citizen of Canada. So much for that. Losing the court battle is followed by losing the field battle. Lethbridge was a disappointment. Instead of heading directly south, we will take Trans-Canada Highway 1 east through Medicine Hat, into Saskatchewan and Swift Current, to Moose Jaw, where we will turn right and head to the USA. (I had to give you all those names of towns because I thought it was an interesting lesson in geography and names). We enter the states through Ft. Portal, manned by one person. We're headed to Bismarck, North Dakota. US 52 leads us to US 83, through Minot and south across the Missouri River. As I mentioned, the Bismarck folks treated us well. Beside the barbecue, they made arrangements for our team to take a steamboat cruise down the "ol' Missouri" River. Another new experience for the players, and it was well received. I can't say that we treated their team well on the field as we picked up a couple of victories. The following day, we were in Mandan, North Dakota, for a game where John struggled early but the team pulled him through offensively. We also toured Fort Lincoln, after which the folks of Mandan put on a dessert gathering for us. Soon, we find ourselves back on I-94, this time headed west to Miles City.

This season's trip to Miles City was a successful one, although we did not win the tournament. However, several positive things happened while we were there. Ernie threw a no-hitter against the Billings Scarlets, 15–0, and Chris shut out Rapid City, 7–0. The big event was that the Cardinals earned their 500th victory, as a team, over Pueblo, Colorado, 17–4. Next, Bobby B. threw a gem of a game, allowing the Billings Royals one run, to vault us into Sunday's finals. A pregame "phantom infield" fired the Cards up as they exploded for four home runs, two triples, and a 15–1 victory. Chris hit two of the home runs. It was a must-win situation, and the Cards were up for it!

What is the phantom infield? The Cardinals' version is simple. We take a regular infield pregame with no baseball. Coach hits a pretend ball to the fielder, and he will make some kind of spectacular play. Some acts that we had were, in the outfield, the worm, an over and under between the centerfielder and right fielder, catches up against the wall. On the last flyball to the center fielder, all the players pretend that the ball is hit so high that it doesn't come down. Two players race out to the fielder with a chair, towel, and large drink, and while the remainder of the fielders finish their routine, he sits in the field. Infielders turn fancy plays, and we even have the first baseman take a bad hop and get knocked out. Two players bring a wheelbarrow out, lift him into it, and wheel him away. Eventually, the ball comes down in center field, and at Denton field, the football press box is in left center, so we have our center fielder climb to the top, reach over, and catch the phantom baseball. The catcher has his own acts. This is the phantom infield! We do all this to Guns N' Roses' "Welcome to the Jungle." Somehow, it's a perfect song for the act.

During the week, a local rancher/baseball fan had invited us to his ranch for a barbecue. One afternoon, we piled into our vans and headed to his ranch, about twenty-nine miles west of Miles City. It was along the Rosebud Creek (read crick for local lingo). He had everything set up for us, including a couple of rifles for the players to shoot at targets and prairie dogs. Some of the players took turns firing the rifles. It was a great gesture by this rancher, who described himself as a big baseball fan, one who liked to watch the Claremont Cardinals when they came to town.

On a similar note, our players were always received well by the Miles City fans. They would come up to our players and tell them, "We're glad to see you back." The interesting part of this is that on many occasions, the player had never been to Miles City, but he "was back," the Cards were back. This season, we only had three players return to Miles City, but this happened every year. The Cardinals headed home to finish the season.

Highlights of the year with a new group of players were these: Chris tied Big Mac's record of thirteen home runs, the team set a record with forty-three home runs, and the Cards picked up their 500th victory as they hit .358 as a team. If we show this power in 1990, it should be an interesting year.

"On the road again, just can't wait to get on the road again." But first, we have two tournaments at home and sixteen games to play. We'll get the 1990 season started with the Ontario Tournament again and will play in a tournament in Fullerton. We will also see, at home, the Billings Scarlets, who are doing their own traveling. Our home field this year is La Verne College. Overall, the Cardinals will probably have the best pitching staff we've had in the past ten seasons. John M. had the lowest era at 1.09 and was undefeated, followed by Ernie R. at 2.67, and led the staff with a 9–0 record, and Bobby B. turned in a 2.77 era. Pat J., in his first year, will go 7–2 with a 3.00 era. He also had a sixteen-strikeout game against Pomona. The staff turned in eight shutouts, and the Cards won thirty-eight of forty-nine games. We had heavy competition in keeping senior players from Claremont High School. A large group of senior men plan a trip to Cabo San Lucas, Mexico, after graduation, every year, and our senior players are pressured into going on that trip This is Keith's last season, and he is part of that group. Keith reports that this happens every year, and every year the senior baseball players opt for Miles City over Cabo! I don't recall losing a player to Cabo. Things look good for the Cards as they prepare for their eleventh road trip.

Flying into Bozeman will be new for Claremont. It's a small international airport in the middle of Montana, just north of Yellowstone. We have to trek up to Lethbridge once again for their tournament. But first, we are scheduled to head east, to Medicine Hat for two games. We play the Medicine Hat Moose Monarchs at Crescent Heights across from the Saskatchewan River. We will stay at the Quality Inn before we head back to Lethbridge. The Cards open the '90 road trip with two victories, including a 6–0 shutout by a combination of Bob S., Paul R., and Bobby B. The road back to Lethbridge, Trans-Canada 3, will take us through Bow Island, home of the Spitz Sunflower Seed giant. One can't find a David and Son's seed anywhere in the Province! The Lethbridge tournament was inundated by rain, and after a few games, the committee made a decision as to who was the winner. It wasn't Claremont.

The next day, we make our way back to the States, stopping in Great Falls for two games on the Fourth of July. Chris and Ernie will team up to throw one-hitter to win the first game, 6–1, and we follow that with another victory. It's the Fourth, so that means barbecue time, and I have all the fixin's needed. Fireworks in Great Falls were under control.

The next morning, we head south on I-15 and pick up I-90 at Butte, then head east toward Bozeman. Before we get to Bozeman, the Cards will make a right turn on Montana 85 and head south along the Gallatin River. The Gallatin River runs north out of Yellowstone National Park, but we are not headed there. About halfway, we will stop where I have reservations for another whitewater trip, half day, down the river. Whitewater trips and riding the rapids have become an exciting adventure for the Cards, and they look forward to it. It's also a way to, in some ways, relax and get away from the ballpark. Our schedules on the road can become demanding. This is also where we will take our annual team picture. Before boarding the raft, and in all the paraphernalia required, we will line up and snap the picture.

You can see the 1990 team picture on the photo pages. After another exciting and wet trip down the river, where a few players went into the drink, which is part of the excitement, the Cards will head to Bozeman, where they will overnight at the Super 8.

The Sheridan Tournament will start on July 5th. We will see Sheridan, Cody, Colorado Springs, and Casper. Patrick J. throws an 8–0 shutout over Colorado Springs to get us started. Steve E. will complete a fete that you won't see too often. He had three hits in one inning against Cody! It was part of a streak of eight consecutive hits for Steve. In that game, we scored sixteen runs in one inning. We finish the tournament as champions. Following the Sheridan tournament, we move our headquarters to the Buckboard Inn in Miles City. The Cards showed power hitting with a lineup dubbed as "The Full Metal Jacket" lineup throughout the tournament. Randy D. batted eighth in the lineup despite his .460 average. Pat shuts out Eugene, Oregon, 11–0, his second straight shutout. The hitters go on a terror, and for the second time in three seasons, the Claremont Cardinals win the Miller Lite-Blue Rock Distributing Invitational Tournament. The Cards head home with two more games to go in the regular season. They handle Pomona and have a non-league game scheduled in El Segundo. Chris R. tosses a 5–0 shutout to end the regular season for the Cards. Claremont sails through the district and enters the Area Playoffs at UCLA's Jackie Robinson Field. In the semifinal game against Camarillo, the Cards have one loss and face a must-win situation. They hand the ball to Ernie. Ernie gets wrapped up in a tight battle but finds himself down 2–1 going into the bottom of the eighth inning. Camarillo immediately loads the bases with nobody out. Bobby B. is brought in, and the little lefty dazzles them by striking out the side, allowing no runs. Randy opens the ninth with a single, Steve doubles over the right fielder's head. An infield out ties the game, and after an intentional pass to Brian L., Bobby S. is looping single caps a four-run outburst, and the Cardinals go on to win, 5–2. That was the climax of the season.

The next day, Santa Monica defeats Claremont and will be going to State. It is an unfortunate ending for a great season. It marks Jorge's last game as a Cardinal. In four years, he will have played 188 games, collected 253 hits, scored 181 runs, and have 217 RBIs. In four seasons, Jorge will have amassed a .382 batting average. He will go on to play at Pepperdine University in California and become a national champion. Randy, Jeff, and Chris each hit a grand slam home run. Randy, in his second season hit .460. Look for him to do better in 1991.

THE YEAR
THAT WASN'T

E arly in 1991, I became aware of the fact that our American Legion league, District 18, Area 6 of California, was facing a decline in membership. Actually there were only three teams: Claremont, Pomona, and Charter Oak. To be an official league and to have an official season culminating in district playoffs, participation in area playoffs, and ability to advance to state playoffs, there must be a minimum of four teams. I was extremely concerned. I even went into Los Angeles to a meeting to see if we could join the league in their area. I was told that we could do that; however, we would have to participate in a schedule that would not allow us to be away for three weeks. Our trip had been planned, and this was not an option. All the years from 1980 on, the biggest reason that we could get away, was that I was the one who made up the entire league schedule. Teams could add any games they wanted around the league games. I started looking around to see if I could find another team. I contacted the Glendora High School coach, who had a summer team for his returning players and was able to convince him to join our league. Now we have four teams, and the district was able to register itself with California.

One of our new players from Claremont High is Justin L., who from this point on will be referred to as Juice. Remember the name Juice. Another key player to join us that year, from our archrival in high school, was Jody N., a shortstop. Remember Jody. We open the season, once again in the Ontario Tournament. We defeat Upland for the championship, 10–4. The Cards are on their way for 1991. Randy D. gets his first home run of the year and is declared tournament MVP. Remember the name Randy! Before we leave on the road trip, the Cards have exploded at the plate! Admittedly, the league was weak, but much of the explosion came against non-league opponents. We had scored thirteen runs in one inning against Glendora and twenty runs in the game. Against Redlands, we had scored twenty-three runs in the game. Seven players had hit fifteen total home runs, including five by Randy and four by Chris R. After losing the first game of the year, Claremont runs off a fifteen-game win streak. The Cards are definitely ready to hit the road.

We open the road trip in Sheridan, Wyoming. During the game, Chris R., our captain, comes to me and tells me that some of their players were calling him some bigoted names. Chris is Hispanic. I told him to not let it affect his game and not to respond. Some of our other players also heard what had been said. We finished the game. As I was standing at home plate talking to their coach, in one of our vehicles heading back to the motel, Randy D. flipped off and cussed at some of their players as his car drove by. This upset the Sheridan players. After we got back to our motel, they showed up and wanted to fight. I was able to quiet the situation by locking down our rooms. Later, I got a letter from the Sheridan booster club asking for an apology and wanting sanction from the American Legion headquarters. They had reported the incident to the American Legion. However, they never mentioned the cause of the incident. I explained our side of the story to the head of the Legion, and he was satisfied after I told him that all the players in the car were fined three days per diem and suspended one game.

The road trip this year will find us in Yellowstone once again. Obviously, I've been there before, but many of this year's players haven't, and that's the purpose of returning. It is a great place to visit. We will take in all the sights, including Old Faithful, Yellowstone Falls, and the "Grand Canyon of Yellowstone, " plus all the bubbly pools. We will also pass through and see the results of some of the big fire that hit Yellowstone three years earlier. It burned nearly 800,000 acres. On the schedule was a whitewater excursion on the Yellowstone River out of Gardner, Montana. Gardner is the north entrance to the park and was a quaint little village at the time. We stayed at a small motel with ten rooms, and we took five of them. The trip down the river was exciting, especially the rapids through Yankee Jim Canyon. We were in two rafts, so while we were in still water, we would have raft fights and try to knock those in the other raft into the river. "Still water runs deep!" After the trip, the Cards headed to a small hamburger stand, The Corral, which was recommended to us, for dinner. They served buffalo burgers, shakes, and fries, so it was perfect for us, and delicious.

During that evening, one of our players, Bobby B. had brought a Ouija board with him, and he took it out. A Ouija board was introduced by the Chinese around AD 1100. It was a board used to communicate with the spirit world through numbers and letters. Bobby had several players attempt to predict their future by moving those numbers and letters around. I don't know how it worked out for them, but Randy reports that, "It scared the f—— out of us!"

After Yellowstone, our goal is to make it to the Rapid City Fire Cracker Tournament. We leave Gardner and head north on US 89, through aptly named Paradise Valley, to Livingston, Montana, where we turn right on I-90 for Billings. We had lunch in Billings and hit the road again. We take I-90 through Sheridan and Buffalo, Wyoming, to Gillette, where we will stay for the night. It always happens around the Fourth of July—players will pick up some fireworks and stash them for future fun. This year is no exception.

In the early evening, Juice has a cherry bomb and tosses it into a room to shake up some teammates. It goes off and damages a carpet—not just any carpet, but a brand-new one installed last week! The manager is furious, and I'm PO'd. The manager tells me that it will cost $300 dollars to get it replaced. I pay the manager the $300 out of team funds and call Juice in to discuss it with me. When we get to Rapid City the next day, I will take him to the closest Western Union and he will wire his parents for the $300 to cover the loss. That is what happened. When we get to Rapid City, we stay east of town in a Days Inn. It was nice enough that when we return to Rapid City, I will book it again. Rapid City is also where we discovered Schlotzsky's, a great sandwich shop.

The ballpark in Rapid City is a big park with a large seating capacity. It could be a minor league park. Beyond the left field fence and on a hill is a large dinosaur. We have great success in Rapid City. Bobby B. throws a 14–0 one hitter against Waite Park, Minnesota, losing a near perfect no-no in the last inning. Ryan strikes out ten batters, in six innings of relief, to pick up a win over Rapid City. In the game of the year, the first game of the tournament, the Cards open the first inning with a two-run home run by Randy D. Bismarck battles to tie the game at four apiece, and with the winning run in scoring position, in the bottom of the seventh, and two outs, Chris R. makes a Willie Mays catch in right-center to end the threat and send it into extra innings. Who leads off for Claremont? Chris! He promptly hits an opposite field home run just as lightning struck, for a climactic moment, and a win. As the song by Lou Christie goes, "Lightning is striking again!" Claremont continues to impress with hitting and pitching, and the Cards go on to win the Fire Cracker Tournament! "Lightning striking again!" It's jacket time! In every tournament that we have won so far, the players receive a jacket instead of a trophy. I think that that is a better way to celebrate your championships, by wearing your "trophy!"

The weather in Rapid City that year was always cloudy and threatening. In one game, as we were playing, all of a sudden they stopped the game and sent the fans and players for cover. The sun was still out! But it didn't take long, and a large gust of wind and great amount of rain and hail came falling. It was a tornado warning! Holy moly! Juice didn't make it under cover in time and was pelted with hail. Still, a campus Doppler saved a lot of trouble.

One night, I heard there was a country Western concert with Willie Nelson, Kris Kristofferson, and some other country Western stars in town. I made announcement to the team that anyone who was interested in going, just let me know and I'll buy the tickets to the concert. I had ten players step up and say they'd go. We left everyone else back at the motel. With Willie and Kris as headliners, it was a great concert. When we got back, I had to straighten out a somewhat immature problem. Other than that, everything was fine.

After the tournament, we took a little sightseeing tour around South Dakota, visiting Deadwood, an old-time gold rush and gambling town. The cemetery has the graves of Wild Bill Hickok and Calamity Jane. Yes, she was a real person. I found a place called Roughlock Falls in Spearfish Canyon, near where a winter camp scene in *Dances with Wolves* was filmed. This area is in the Black Hills of South Dakota. We took our team picture at the falls. We also visited Mount Rushmore, and I took a few players who wanted to go down the road on US 365 to visit the Crazy Horse monument outside Custer City, South Dakota. So far, the Cards have had a great season, as we head to our annual Miles City Tournament.

Once again, the road trip will end in Miles City. Claremont will continue hitting the ball and getting great pitching. So far, four players have hit grand slam home runs: Scott F., Randy D., Marty M., and Jody N. The team will have hit fifty homers. Ten players will have a batting average over .300, led by Randy's .500 season average and Steve's .464 season average. Both Jody and Marty M. have turned in over .400 averages. On the bump, Pat J. will be undefeated with a 9–0 record, Chris 7–0, and Bobby B. 8–1. The season earned run average for pitchers is 2.81, and they have held their opponents to a .211 batting average. Chris will throw a 11–0 two-hit shutout at the Las Vegas Valley team, but the Cards will falter in the championship game, and with all these numbers, the tournament will become a disappointment. I am going to tell this story despite Jeff S.'s cry of, "What happens at the Buckboard stays at the Buckboard."

On the last day in Miles in the afternoon, I went to the park to watch a game. Most of the players stayed "back at the ranch." Apparently, in the afternoon, Jody had gone to get some ice at the machine, and while he was there, met a young woman. Jody is outgoing, so they began to talk. She told him that she was a stripper in Vegas, here with her husband. Forward-talking Jody suggested that she should come strip for the team in one of the rooms in the evening. Well, it was getaway day, and I suggested that everyone pack up tonight because we would be leaving for Billings and the airport in the morning. So I'm doing just that, packing, in my room that night. I decide to check up on the rest of the team, and I go next door. Nobody there. It's quiet. Down to the next room. Nobody there. Repeat! Finally, as I'm walking past room 260, I hear music wafting out of the window, so I go in. I see Juice sitting on the edge of a bed with the stripper doing her thing right in front of him, and the rest of the team enjoying what is going on. Coach Mike is standing on a bed in the corner taking pictures! I have to say, she was not entirely unclothed while doing gyrations in her dance. Her husband was close by. I thought about screaming and hollering at the players, but that wouldn't accomplish anything, so I asked Chris R., our captain, to come outside with me, and I told him he had five minutes to make sure this was over. I left, and it was. For the players, it was a seized opportunity. This has been remembered as Club 260 by the Claremont Cards. I wonder if Coach Mike still has the pictures.

We get ready to fly home the next day. At the airport, we start to check in. There is a sign reading, "No jokes about bombs, they will be taken seriously and violators will be prosecuted to the fullest extent of the law." Well, apparently one of our players couldn't read, or decided to challenge the rule, and tossed a volleyball he had past the baggage screener and onto the conveyor belt. The employee got very upset, and Scott C. didn't help the matter by exclaiming, "Yeah, it's a bomb." All bejesus broke loose. The supervisor was called, and I spent fifteen minutes trying to keep us out of jail, proving it was a volleyball, with no harm intended. Finally, after getting a very stern warning, the supervisor allowed us to catch our plane. I was the last one on board.

When we returned home, we had one more game with Charter Oak. But the news was not good. While we were out of town, Glendora had dropped out of the league, leaving only three teams. That disqualifies us from any state playoffs, and we can't have a district playoff. The season is over. What a huge disappointment! There was nothing we could do. An appeal to the state American Legion proved useless. This was a great team, but there was no way to prove it. Several players were upset about the situation, especially our captain, Chris. We just had to be happy about the great season we had and the fun we've had on the road.

THE DUEL

During the high school season, I will pay attention to how well some of the players on other teams in our league are doing. I knew about Matt W., the Bonita pitcher, but I sent my coach, Mike to the game to watch him anyway. Mike came back raving about a player, but it wasn't Matt! It was their second baseman. Coach Mike said, "This guy was all over the field, directing traffic on almost every play." Who was that? Brock W.! I made contact with him as well as Matt, and we were able to pick up both players for the 1992 season. Both players were very excited. However, I found out early in the season that Brock had a flaw. He couldn't shoot pool very well, but we will work around that!

On the 24th of June, we fly into Billings. We are 20–3, as we leave for our thirteenth road trip. Who would have thought that I'd still be doing this? Yes, we've had some crazy things happen, but I have never bailed any player out of jail, and any damages we've caused have been small and innocent. I put Juice's cherry bomb damage last year in the category of stupid, but it was satisfactorily resolved. We take off as an exciting baseball team and have played some already memorable games. The Cards swept the Ontario tourney with a victory over Alta Loma. Juice is MVP of the tournament with eight hits in eleven at bats.

Starting the second game of the season, Jody N. is put into the leadoff spot in the lineup, and he goes on a terror! Heading into the road trip, he is hitting .462, including three home runs, all leading off the game for the Cards. As a leadoff hitter, he has 24 RBIs. Surprisingly, we've shut out a usually strong West Covina team three consecutive times, and we've done it with five different pitchers. Matt W. went all the way, Joe C. and John M. pitched minimum six innings, each for wins. Jeff B. and Ryan R. contributed. We are in Billings once again to participate in their tournament. Billings has been good to us, and it has been easy to say yes, we'll be back. Laurel, Montana, just west of Billings, is our first opponent. We built up a ten-run lead in the top of the fifth behind Chris R. In the bottom of the inning, Chris falters slightly, and John M. does a major job in closing. Matt takes care of Aurora, Colorado, with help from Juice's home run, double, and 4 RBIs. Joe struggles in the rain against Taylorsville, Utah. Jeff B. throws a four-hit shutout against Idaho Falls to win 12–0. That is it for Billings this season.

The next day is travel day, and our destination is Rapid City. I decide to take the scenic route instead of the interstates, so we take I-90, 54 miles down the road to US 212, right near the Custer Battlefield and the Crow Indian Reservation. We stop to visit the battlefield and then head east on US 212. It's a two-lane road, but this ain't California! There are not very many vehicles on the highway, so the going is easy and fast. The road takes us through one of the oldest cow towns in America, Belle Fourche (pronounced bell foosh), South Dakota. By 1890, the town had become the world's largest livestock shipping point, using the railroad that passed through it, going east. A few thousand carloads of cattle from Kansas, Texas, and Montana were shipped east each month. Belle Fourche became the agricultural center of the three-state area. Twenty miles north of the city is the geographical center of the United States. US 212 meets up with I-90 in Spearfish, and we finish the trip on the Interstate, driving through Sturgis, home of the famous motorcycle rally.

Our first game is with Rapid City Post 22, the most well-known team in South Dakota. Matt is not on, allowing eight runs, striking out just two in four plus innings, as we lose, 11–3. It will be his worst game of the season. We will see Post 22 down the road. Joe rights the ship the next day as he throws a complete 9–0 shutout over Waite Park, Minnesota. In a surprise start, Juice gets the nod to face Burnsville, Minnesota. In a surprise finish, he goes all the way for a 5–3 victory, driving in two runs on two sacrifice fly balls. In the third inning of the game, I took a stroll out to see the umpire in the infield. He charged me with a trip to the mound, and in the ensuing discussion, I was ejected from the game. I just wanted to talk to him. Juice's complete game gave our regular starting rotation a welcome respite. John M. takes over the next day against another Las Vegas team, Bonanza, and gives up one run on four hits for a win. On the Fourth of July, Ryan can't get out of the third inning against a team from Regina, Saskatchewan. That kills our chances for any tournament title. We watch the Rapid City fireworks show near the dinosaur on the hill. In the final game of the tournament for the Cards, Matt is back on the mound for a great pitcher's duel against Colorado Springs. After seven innings, it is a 2–2 tie. The game goes into the tenth inning and Juice and Matt B. open the inning with back-to-back doubles to break the tie. Cards score three more and win 6–2. Matt W. goes all the way, ten innings, and the final three outs are strikeouts giving him eighteen in the game! On to Billings and some more excitement.

It's three days before we play in Miles City, so how about a little detour to Dickinson, North Dakota? We have a two-game meeting with them at Dickinson State. Out of Rapid City, we pick up US 85 and go straight north until we get to I-94. A right-hand turn and thirty miles put us in Dickinson. Chris S. has the assignment in the first game, and the team picks up thirteen runs on sixteen hits, and Chris sails 13–2. Juice drives in five runs. In the second game Jeff B. throws a shutout 12–0 in five innings. He allows two hits. The meeting turns out to be a walk in the park! The Cards' first game in Miles City is against a team from Calgary, Canada. The Cards build up an 8–4 lead going into the bottom of the sixth, but Joe C. has trouble getting three outs. With the tying run in scoring position and two out, Matt W. comes in to get the final out on a strikeout. It is Matt's nineteenth strikeout in 10 1/3 innings—keep that in mind! Time limit is called, and the Cards escape with the victory, 8–7. We can go back to the Buckboard, relax, sleep in, and hang by the pool the next day.

Fort Worth, Texas, is our next opponent, in a 5:00 p.m. game. After Juice's complete game victory in Rapid City, I give him the start. Claremont has what has become a typical late inning rally and scores five runs in the bottom of the seventh, but leaves the tying runs on base as Jody grounds out to short. Cards lose 8–6, but it's not all Juice's doing. They make six errors in the game, allowing only five earned runs. Maybe the problem was too much hanging by the pool in the early afternoon. At any rate, I was irate! I hold a team meeting in my room and go off on the team in general. Let me quote Jeff on the meeting, "I remember counting on both hands Coach dropping f-bombs. It was almost like he was making up words that included the f-word. *Helbs* was on a good one. I tried so hard not to laugh, not at the fact that we were in some kind of trouble, but just the new vocabulary that was invented!" Let's hope my point was well taken.

The next day, we have a 12:30 afternoon game, but the weather is threatening. We play Lethbridge, and the game gets started just after 12:30 in the afternoon. John M. is on the mound, with Ramon D. behind the plate. In the fourth inning, the weather catches up with us, and we will have a one-hour-and-forty-five-minute delay, during which the tarp was brought out and some players decided to have some fun running and sliding on the tarp. When the game resumes, John continues to shut down the Elks 9–0. It is the ninth shutout thrown by the Cardinals this season and sets a team record. (You gotta believe that in all these years, statistics have been kept and records recorded). Next up, El Segundo.

The duel of the Californians has become a classic in the tournament, and this year it will top all games between the two teams. Matt W. is the starter for the Cards against one of El Segundo's aces.

The tournament knows how to draw a crowd because they schedule this game for 8:00 p.m. The game is delayed for one and a half hours because of prior weather and starts a few minutes after 9:30 p.m. El Segundo picks up a scratch run in the first and adds to that with a run in the third. Through six innings, the Cards have less than amassed two hits total, although they failed to cash in three errors. Down 2–0, going into the top of the seventh inning, Ken M. opens with a single and Ramon D. walks. Eric B. moves them over with a perfect sacrifice bunt, bringing up pitcher Matt, who is no fluke at the plate, having hit .360 all season. Matt hits a drive to left field, which falls into the fielder's glove but drives in a run. Jody is safe on an error, which allows Claremont to tie the score. The top of the seventh is over when Jody is thrown out trying to steal second, but the Cards have tied the game. Matt gets in trouble in the bottom of the inning, but two strikeouts gets him out of it. Claremont is up and out in the eighth. Now the question is, should I send Matt out in the bottom of the eighth? His father is in the stands so, the three of us converge to discuss the situation. His father is opposed to sending him out to the mound. Matt is adamant that he wants to continue. I'm in the middle, and I'm the one who has to pull the strings. I don't want to hurt a top player. Matt wins and pitches the eighth, picking up three more strikeouts. That is 14 Ks, and remember, that takes a lot of pitches. We are keeping the pitch count. More blanks in the ninth, and tenth, and after each inning we have the same confab with Matt winning each time. But I'm getting ready to take charge and shut him down. In the top of the eleventh inning, Ramon D. and Eric B. get on base to start the inning. Matt is due up, but this is no time to pinch hit, since we know he can hit, and the top of the lineup, Jody is next. Matt singles to drive in the go ahead run. Claremont scores four more runs and is up 7–2. After pleading hard with his father, Matt returns to the mound and finishes the game with twenty strikeouts! His catcher, Eric, says, "Matt was as strong in the eleventh as he was in the first."

He showed it with 9 strikeouts in the last four innings, and with the Rapid City game and one relief appearance in between, he records thirty-nine strikeouts in 21 1/3 innings! His father is relieved, I'm relieved and I know Matt is elated, as well as relieved. His pitch count for the game was 178! I don't know of too many coaches who would allow this, but my thoughts included the fact that Matt was big and strong, and this was the end of the season, so he should be in top-of-the-line shape. He would not have pitched the twelfth, I'm sure, but glad it didn't happen. To finish, Brock is the offensive player of the game with four hits, including a two-run single in the eleventh to break the game open. Later on, after Matt had become a professional player, he was quoted as saying, "The El Segundo game was the most fun game I've ever experienced." Kenny M., Jody, and Matt make the all-tourney team. Two days later, we lose the championship game to El Segundo, 6–3. For this road trip, we were 12–5.

One day, I was walking downtown and happened to pass the Montana Bar. Outside was a plaque indicating that the Montana Bar was on the Historical Registry List. I went in to find out about it. The bar had been established in 1908 and had been frequented by Teddy Roosevelt, among many other personalities. The actual bar had been brought up the Missouri River and delivered by mule train to Miles City. This historical place sounded to me like a good place for a team picture, so I asked the manager if we could take it at the bar. He said, "Sure, but come in the morning." So the next morning, I had the players dress in uniform and we took our 1992 team picture at the Montana Bar. I made sure they knew the history, so when their parents saw the picture, they could explain it to them.

Flying home was a little shaky with some air turbulence, but we landed in Ontario safely. There was one league game remaining with West Covina, after a one-week break. Go to the beach, but be back for practice in three days. We had qualified for district playoffs, so I wanted to use this game for our pitchers to get back into the groove. John, Jeff, Joe, Matt, Ryan each got some innings to pitch, and the five of them held West Covina to two runs for a 3–2 victory. John went three innings allowing both runs. Jeff threw two innings, and Joe went two innings, getting credit for the win (9–3). Matt and Ryan each threw one inning. As fate would have it, we open the district playoffs against West Covina. In four games this season, they had scored a total of two runs, off our pitching. In this game, we explode for twenty runs on twenty-two hits behind Matt, to win 20–4. Jody did his early season "thing" by opening the game with a home run, his sixth of the year. He collected three more hits and had seven runs batted in. Brock was 3–4 with two runs and three RBIs, and Matty B. went 3–5 and scored four times. The Cards get a forfeit win over Pomona because they didn't have enough players. They wanted to start the game with eight players, because they had some players participating in other games. District officials said no and declared a forfeit. The championship game is also with Pomona. This time, they were ready—or were they? Matt is on the hill, Claremont builds up a 9–2 lead, and Ryan takes over in the seventh. Final score, 16–2. Jody collects five hits and scores five runs, and Matt picks up his seventh consecutive hit and ninth win. Claremont is district champ for the fifth straight year. The Cards are going to Area Playoffs at UCLA again! In the opener, John M. struggles, and the Cards fall 13–2 to Newbury Park. Yes, that was quite a shock! Not half the shock as the second game, which was another pitcher's battle in which the Cards lose in eleven innings, after scoring in the top of the eleventh to take the lead, 4–3. The winning run came in on an error by our shortstop. Game, set, match! An ugly way to end another great year.

Jody leads the team with a .445 average, 53 runs scored, and 44 RBIs. He also had 21 extra base hits, including 6 home runs. Brock follows with a .418 average, and Juice checks in with a steady .358. Do you want to hear Matt's stats on the mound? Matt threw 94 innings, struck out 123, and turned in a 1.34 era. He had a 10–2 record and had a 10-inning complete game followed by an 11-inning complete game. Take a break. Time to get ready for next year.

A CHANGE
IN SCENERY

I n the '93 season, some things will change. First, the Cards will have several new additions to the roster. To do this, there will be a try-out at Claremont McKenna College, where more than fifty players show up. I can only have a roster of eighteen and must stick with that because of insurance. Seven players will return from last season, which leaves room for eleven new players. Every player out there had the ability to play on the team. After a week of agonizing, I finally had to make some decisions. The night of the phone calls was painful to me because I had to tell good players that I had no spot for them on the team.

The Cardinals open the season in Las Vegas. There are several high schools in Vegas, and most of them sponsor an American Legion team in the summer. In the tourney, we will play three of the teams. The Cards head north on I-15 over the Cajon Pass, and with miles of the windswept Mojave Desert flashing by, passing little known set-tlements of Yermo, Baker, and Mountain Pass, the border town of Primm, and Jean until they get to Las Vegas. Jean is the home of the Southern Nevada Prison. They have a 5:00 p.m. game against

Chapparal. Jeff B., who is returning from last year, gets the honors to start the first game of the year. He takes a 6–2 lead into the sixth and gets into trouble giving up three runs. Greg R. comes in and cleans up the mess, for a save. In the second inning, Jeff B. grounds into a double-play to end the inning. What makes his at bat significant is that it is the 30,000 official at bat for the Cardinals. (I told you earlier, we keep statistics!). After the game, we check into Sam's Town for our stay in Vegas. I wasn't concerned about players gambling at the tables or machines. If they were successful in having some fun, more power to them. Greg S. throws the second game and goes all the way for a 9–4 win. The Cards finish the tournament against an old foe, the Strawberries, Las Vegas Valley. Nick gets the win as Matt W. gets 2 doubles, 2 RBIs, and scores 2 runs, in a 9–3 outing. The Cards use everybody in the tournament, and they look good to go! They come home for the Ontario tournament. Matt will pitch the first game in Ontario, and in a tight one, he finishes with a 3–2 victory. Brian D. has a 3–3 day at the plate and drives in the third run. Our first loss comes at the hands of Chino, 4–2, but we will roar back and score 19 runs the following night. We will open league, scoring 4 runs in the eighth to tie Pomona, and a run in the tenth for the win. Chris's bases loaded triple in the eighth was the big hit. The season has started, and I like what I see.

The Cards have built up a 15–2 record before leaving for the road. In the game before our departure, Steve B. scored five times in a victory over West Covina and Matt W. will have a 4–0 record. The team is coming together on the field and within themselves. It has developed a great camaraderie as almost everyone has been dubbed a nickname. In the game, before we left for the road, as I read the score sheet, the lineup read, "Dr. Dre, Knocker, the Juiceman, Bart, Willie, Sushi, Door, Navajo, Ogre." Replacements included "T-bone, Beam me Up, and Orca." Players took care of the score sheet, so I had to decipher who was whom! I liked it, because I like nicknames. Somehow, it brings a group together. I don't know how Brian B. escaped, but he'll get his later.

Claremont is ready to hit the "wild blue yonder!" First stop, Lethbridge. Matt W.—or should I say Sushi—will not be with us for the first few games, because he is at a showcase camp in the east. How he got that name, I do not know. In the army, the sarge hollers, "Left, right, left." We started off on the wrong foot and dropped one to Lethbridge 8–3. But this is not part of the tournament. Greg S. straightens the situation out with a shutout over Twin Falls, Idaho. After a double-digit victory over Clarkston, Washington, we let one slip in the last inning to Calgary, 13–12. Matt is returning to the Cards from his showcase, but I have to pick him up at the airport. Lethbridge has an airport, but that would make it an international flight, so he flies into Great Falls. I go pick him up. It's 105 kilometers to the border on Alberta 4, and 117 miles on I-15 to GTF, or approximately 182 miles one way. When we get back to Lethbridge, Brian D. is on the mound facing Taiwan. He holds his own, but that game is called after seven in a 4–4 tie. The next day, Matt W. handles a team from Orange County, California 8–3. The highlight of the tournament for the Cards is Matt N.'s, no-hitter against hometown Lethbridge! It was called after five innings with the score 9–0. But it was a no-no! Again, rain plays havoc with the tournament and ends it prematurely. We leave on Trans-Canada 3 east toward Medicine Hat for a scheduled game. That's a nine-inning affair that four pitchers take care of in a 12–0 game. Nick started it and went five innings so he gets the win.

Once again, we hop on Trans-Canada 1 for Moose Jaw, Saskatchewan, and make a right on Alberta 39 to Estevan and the border. I find US 52 and take it southeast to Minot, where we will play in their tournament. Five miles outside of Minot, Bill W. says he has to make a pit stop.

"What? We're only five miles out of town. Can't you wait?"

"Nope!"

I pull over to the side of the road, and we open both front and back doors for Bill's privacy and he does his thing! You couldn't do that at home, only because you wouldn't be able to find a place to pull over, and you'd be blocking traffic. Here, outside of Minot, there is no traffic. Problem solved! Some players asked me, "Why are we going to Minot?"

My answer was simple, "Why not?"

Minot! The city is home to Minot Air Force Base. Corbett Field is an interesting field in that both dugouts are behind home plate, one on the left side, one on the right. Also there is a downward slope in the outfield and a large building looming over right field. Greg S. gives up three hits and doesn't allow a run in a 14–0 whitewash of Dickinson. Bill hits a three-run homer to open the game up in the fourth. Rob C. has three hits and scores every time. In the second game, against Jamestown, ND, Scotty gets us started by popping one with two out in the second, and Brian D. finishes with a 9–1 win. Matt N. gets the Pierre, South Dakota, team and holds them for a victory. Ogre gets a three-run home run in the fifth to settle that argument. In the final game, Nick can't get out of the first inning, and we lose 8–3. The game was shortened to five innings because of rain. I'm sure we would have rallied to win, but it wasn't in the Cards. It continues to rain, and the next day, all games were canceled. While we are hanging around, I find a gym to play some basketball. With the tournament called off that day, we leave Minot. The Cards head south on US 83 crossing the Missouri River and Lake Sakakawea and do some zigzagging until they find ND 49 and I-94. heading west, toward Miles City. Cruising through Dickinson, they are on their way.

THE CRASH

The Cardinals are traveling in three vehicles this year. A fifteen-passenger van, a minivan, and a four-door sedan. I am driving the passenger van, while Coach Bill is driving the mini and Coach Ryan is driving the sedan. My rule on the road is that you don't pass me or play any kind of car tag games. Coach Bill is a twenty-two-year-old player on the college team where I coach. Coach Ryan is a young ex-player on the Cardinal team as well as the high school team. I asked him to join us because I wanted someone specifically in charge of the pitchers, and he pitched for us a few years ago. The passenger van has been named, in the past, as the "rookie van," because the youngest players were assigned to ride in it with me. "Mule Train!" The other vehicles were manned by various members of the "veterans." Riding in the minivan was an ace pitcher and both catchers, as well as another player. I had the youngest players, including our hard-hitting short-stop, Willie. Ryan had the rest of the players, about four. This was the fifth of July, and several players had stashed extra fireworks in their gear to use elsewhere. We are cruising along I-94 west of Dickinson, North Dakota, when we pass a semi-truck. As we pass, Willie, sitting in the back of my van, decides to light a firecracker and throw it out the window in front of the semi. I can only speculate as to what the semi driver was thinking, "a bunch of kids letting loose!" So he begins to pull over and let everybody go by. Now, I'm watching this entire scene in my rearview mirror, and I decide to pull over. Coach Bill is following my rule, and he too pulls over right behind me, while Coach Ryan sails by and pulls over in front of me. Coach Bill's minivan just clears the semi, which can't stop quick enough, and it crashes into the rear of the minivan. The van careens down an embankment, and as I watch, I'm imagining a rollover and possibly one or two players killed. This is when Coach Bill goes into action. He is from San Diego, and has driven Baja races in Mexico before. (Google Baja Races.) He immediately jerks the steering wheel and guides the van, nose first, down the embankment. He then yanks the wheel and straightens the van out parallel to the highway. Disaster has been avoided. Now to deal with the semi driver. He has pulled beyond us and parked in front of us. I am not very happy and shied from talking to him, because it is all our fault. He comes storming back toward me, and we meet, no handshake. He immediately tells me that his company has a policy that if a driver gets into an accident, the driver will be fired. Well, this wouldn't be fair, so I tell him to give me his company address and I will immediately send them a letter absolving him of any responsibility. He does that. I am very apologetic. Someone has alerted the North Dakota Highway Patrol, and they have arrived. The officer takes a report from both of us, and seeing that no one was injured, he leaves. The driver gets into his truck, and he leaves also. The rest of us survey the scene and determine that the minivan can be driven, so we spend time pushing the van back onto the interstate. I start collecting all the fireworks that I can, hoping I can get all of them, knowing that I probably won't, despite some very threatening consequences. When we finally get to Miles City and pull into the Buckboard, I want to hide our damages, so I tell Coach Bill to back it into a spot where no one can see the rear end. Miles City is a small town, and any and everything is news and winds up in the newspaper. I didn't want that publicity. I quickly call Thrifty car rental in Billings, and the next morning they had picked up our van and left us a new van for the rest of the trip. We will settle with them when we get back to Billings. This accident was the most scary event on any trip so far, and it was caused by fireworks.

After we settled in at the Buckboard, I made another check for fireworks. I know, and I don't believe the players realized, that when we leave from Billings, they would not be allowed on the plane. Anyway, we have a tournament to win! We open up with Miles City. Matt W. is on the mound, his first appearance in Miles City after last season's eleven-inning adventure. He and Nick will split six innings of work in a 14–2 ball game. This game featured three home runs by three players who would be your last guess. In the third inning, our eighth and ninth hitter, Scotty C. and Matt W., hit back-to-back bombs. Leading off the sixth, Matt N. hit a solo home run that started a five-run inning and literally put the game away for us. In the second game versus Las Vegas Knights, we escape with a run in the seventh on a hit by Jeff S. scoring Juice. Matty picks up the win in relief of Greg S. In game 3 versus Colorado Springs, Juice goes 3 for 3 with 3 RBIs, including a home run, helping Jeff B. to a victory. Matt N. is pitching against Pleasant Grove, Utah, and enjoys the support of 14 runs on 17 hits for a 14–5 win. Juice is at it again, with 4 RBIs on 4 hits. Bill W. scores four times. Jeff S. ends a 21-game hitting streak. He'll start another one! We are 4–0 and have scored forty runs and allowed sixteen in those games. Next up will be the Eugene, Oregon, Pepsi Challengers. Greg R. starts on the mound, but my plan is to not have any pitcher throw too many pitches, because I know the next day we probably will have to play two games. I'm hoping I can get by with using three pitchers. So of course, in a scheduled seven-inning game, we go eleven! Worse, Eugene had tied the game up with two runs in the seventh, 3–3. Brian D. has it easy in the ninth and tenth, but that's all she wrote! He opened the eleventh by walking the bases loaded. The next day is Sunday, and we will play a semifinal game versus El Segundo. Another home run by Juice as well as a double, and a rally-starting triple by Rob, in the fifth, helps us escape with a five-inning game called because of a ten-run rule. Matty has thrown a limited amount of pitches in three innings. A rematch with Eugene

Pepsi-Challengers is our reward. This game will be the 999th game for the Cards since they were created in 1972. Greg S. starts the game for us. Two runs in the second by Eugene puts us in an early hole. In the top of the third, Scotty singles, with two out, Rob singles followed by Steve's single to load the bases. Juice is up, and on a 1–1 pitch hits a triple to right-center driving in three runs. Matty is on the bench, and I scramble to get him up to loosen up. Jeff S. helps with a run scoring single, and the Cards lead, 4–2. When we take the field, Matty is on the mound and shuts Eugene out the rest of the way. I must say, that Greg S. was not happy about the change, and I didn't blame him. He was an excellent pitcher for us. One more thing. I've been talking about hitting and pitching, but in this game some great defense helped us out. Rob made two sparkling plays at second base, and Jeff S. made a great catch in right field to keep us out of trouble. The Claremont Cardinals have won the Miles City Tournament three times! Juice, Matty, and Jeff S. make all-tournament team. Our 1993 team picture is taken on the field with our winning jackets. Tomorrow it is Delta on the way home.

The Cardinals arrive home with a 29–6 record and two tied games, but they have seventeen more games to play! They have less than twenty-four hours after they get off the plane, before they must play a conference road game against Pomona. Needless to say, they sleepwalk through this game in a 5–1 loss on four hits. Against Arcadia, four days later, they can't hold onto a 5–0 lead in the seventh inning and lose, 6–5. Somebody jump-start Jeff S.! They apparently did, because he hits two home runs against West Covina driving in five runs in a 12–3 win for Greg's seventh victory. Jeff S. will finish the season with a fifteen-game hitting streak, hitting .479 in the streak with 30 RBIs. Matt N. finishes the regular season with 4–1 win over Charter Oak, leading into the district playoffs. The Cards open with a 6–2 victory over Pomona, but fall the next day to West Covina 8–6. That puts them in a hole, but Greg S. shuts the door on Pomona once again, 9–3. Steve is 5–5 in that game. Claremont will face West Covina, and the Cards will have to beat them twice. Nick takes care of the first game with offensive help from Jeff S., with three hits and four RBIs. Jeff B. gets involved in a pitcher's battle, and the Cards enter the ninth inning up 3–0. An eight-run ninth inning capped by Juice's two-run home run seals the deal for Jeff, Juice, and the Cardinals, 11–0. They will be headed to UCLA once again for the Area Playoffs. Matt W. will get the start against Westchester. Is he nervous? No way! He has placed a tube up through the back of his uniform and into the back of his cap and is walking around before the game squirting fans, teammates, anyone else he sees, as they look around trying to determine where it came from. He would walk away with a smirk on his face. After he got me, it took me fifteen minutes to figure out where it came from! Matt was ready! His long, lanky body is loose as well as his mind. He throws a three-hit shutout, and the Cards back him with ten runs on twelve hits. Because of the ten-run rule, he only goes eight innings. Steve and Jeff S. are at it again, each with three hits and three RBIs. Ventura becomes the next opponent, and Greg S. throws the next shortened game 13–3. Five players bang out two or more hits, and Steve, Greg's battermate in this game, again drives in three. Seventeen more hits and thirteen more runs are enough to get beyond Woodland Hills, although the Cards had to play nine innings. Jeff B. was the benefactor of this barrage. Keeping the ball down and away allowed for four double plays to keep Jeff out of some trouble. Bill, Juice, and Matt N. joined the hit parade. Bill and Juice each had three runs batted in, and Matt N. had four hits. A 3–0 record in the Area Playoffs puts the Cards in the championship, needing to lose two games. Westchester has fought their way back and will be the Cards' opposition in the championship. With Matt W. on the mound, the Cardinals need a two-run rally in the ninth to tie the game. They get a two out, two run double by Steve and send the game into the tenth. In the top of the tenth, Brian D. gives up a two out solo home run, and that run holds up. Cards lose 5–4, forcing a second game for the championship. Matt N. is the Cards starter. He gives up two runs on two solo home runs, while Jeff S. collects a three-run home run in the fifth to put the Cards ahead. They will pick up two more in the seventh, as Matt N. gets his seventh win on the mound, 6–4. Five days later, Claremont gets ready to drive up to Yountville once again. They'll take with them a 40-10-2 record.

I honestly have to attribute some of the success of the team this season, to the ability to remain loose when the situation could call for some major seriousness. Hyperventilation was not part of our attack. Matt W's squirt gun effort before a big game, and Brian B.'s antics before a game in Yountville (see picture) are just two examples. Nevertheless, in the first game, Matt W. allows three runs in eight innings, and the Cards open State Playoffs with a twenty-hit explosion against Union City. Rob, Bill W., and Eric each have four hits, Jeff S. has three hits, including two doubles, and three RBIs. Bill W. had four hits, including three doubles. His last at bat, in the ninth inning, was a two-run double, and also the 10,000th hit in Cardinal history. After striking out twice, Chris joins in with his ninth home run. Final score is 12–4.

In game 2, the Cards should have saved some hits and should have saved some runs as they are ten-run-ruled 12–1 by Fairfield. How weird is it to be on the other side? Claremont faces Union City again in what becomes the final game of the season. Some hitting is back on track as Jeff S. picks up four hits. Bill W. and Juice each homer, but it will not be enough as the Cards drop their second loss, 13–7. Jeff S. finishes the season with a .449 average, 66 RBIs, and 59 runs scored. He also set a team record with 31 doubles. Juice is right behind with a .442 average, and he has stolen 30 bases in 31 attempts. Matt W. turns in a 13–0 record with two saves and 125 Ks in 99 2/3 innings, and a 0.99 era. His career is just beginning. Before we were to leave, the California chairman had asked for a ride to the airport, since we had our own vehicles. I left Borman field and forgot to wait for him. He got ahold of me while we were eating in a restaurant in town. I had to go back to get him. He wasn't happy! Season's over, but another great year for the Claremont Cardinals.

A ROCKY ROAD

"Baseball is like fishing. In baseball, you try to lure the hitter with different pitches. In fishing, you try to lure different fish with various lures!" That is Nick A.'s philosophy on pitching. Nick pitched for us last year, so we are counting on him to pitch well for us this season. This also makes him our resident psychologist. The year 1994 should be interesting. The Cards will have another big turnover. Both catchers will be gone and replaced by Doug B. and Lenny S. Matt W. has left, to be heard from by the Angels, and later the Brewers. Juice has moved on, causing a big hole in the lineup. Another power-hitting outfielder, Jeff S., is gone. Rob C., who gave us consistent hitting and slick fielding in the infield, will be back. Brian D. returns in the outfield and on the hill. Chris H. S. will be back at first base. Bill W., a huge part of our offense and team, returns for another season, but we will be counting on Chris C., Mike J., Troy K., Jeff P., Dave R., Adrian S., Rich D., Lawson R., and Darren W. to help pick up where we left in '93. As we get the season started, I get a feeling this team will need a psychologist!

Let's take the first games of the season, for example. Greg is our choice as opening pitcher. Bill W. hits a leadoff home run in the top of the fifth against Charter Oak, at their place. It is only one of two hits we get for the game, but it is enough, as the Cardinals, behind Greg S., open the conference and the season with a 1–0 victory. Brian D. picked up a scratch single for the other hit in the eighth. Greg allows four hits in his nine-inning masterpiece. However, the Cards show some lack of discipline that must be squelched. Doug B., our catcher, misses three signs and is fined $2 each. After the game, during my postgame talk, Greg becomes very disturbing, causing others to pay more attention to him than myself. Another fine. If we are going to become a solid unit, as in the past, we must square things now.

The Ontario Tournament is next. Jeff P. will pick up a win over Chino, 8–6. During the game, Chino had a base runner streaking toward home plate where our catcher, Doug, was waiting with the ball. High school had changed the rules about crashing into the catcher, making it illegal. But American Legion had not. I failed to make sure our catchers knew this, and the Chino runner barreled into Doug and sent him flying. It was legal. Doug survived, but I felt bad. Doug is not big in stature, but he is big in grit! With Troy K. making his debut for the Cards on the mound, Claremont returns to discipline problems in the form of a lack of concentration. Rich D., our left fielder, drops a routine fly ball in the first inning, and in the same inning, third baseman, Mike J., throws to the plate on a ground ball when no one was trying to score. These silly gaffs caused the Cards to give up eight runs in the first. We never recovered in a game, called because of time limit. Frankly, this is not a good start for the season. However, as I have mentioned, in the past, that this is why we play in the early season Ontario Tournament. Let's get things ironed out!

It has become harder than it should. By the time we hit the road, we are 11-8-1. We've had missed signs, a player ejected for language, a player yanked from the game for back talk, a player missing from a game with no excuse, and a player injured because he was arm wrestling on the bench. Rob also had to go to the hospital because he was beaned at the plate. He was all right, though. And we were shut out in back-to-back games for the first time ever! There were some positives, though. Greg was 4–0, Troy was settling in as a hitter and holding his own on the mound, Rob has yet to make an error in the season as a middle infielder, and Bill has become a key part of our lineup again, as expected. It looks like these are the guys we are going to have to rely on.

In the last game before we left on our trip, the players dedicated the game to Bobby S., an ex-player from 1988–1989, who was popular and had just been diagnosed with leukemia. Chris C. and Bill W. pitched in with multiple hits and multiple RBIs to lead the way for a 11–4 win. That makes it a positive send-off for our trip.

On June 22, we board a plane in Ontario for Billings, Montana. We are headed to tournaments in Williston, North Dakota, Rapid City, Miles City. When we get to Billings, I take a shuttle to Thrifty Car Rental to get our ground transportation. After loading up players and gear, the Cards head east on I-94 along the Lewis and Clark Trail. We pass Pompey's Pillar, where Lewis and Clark etched their names on a rock pillar along the river in 1806. I-94 takes us through Miles City and east to Glendive, where we make a left on Montana 16, north to Sydney and Fairview and the North Dakota border. Turning east again, we will be on ND 200 to US 85, which will take us north to Williston. This will be our first time in Williston.

The ballpark in Williston is at the Aafedt Stadium near the Williston Community College. Our first game is with Escanaba, Michigan. Jeff is on the "bump" but implodes in the third for six runs, and the Cards can't catch up, a 10–3 loss. In game 2, Greg S. holds the hometown team, the Williston Keybirds, to two runs, but a run allowed by Chris H. S. in the seventh, knocks us out, 3–2. In game 3, against Laurel, we give up seven in the fourth on the way to a 12–10 loss. Adrian's homer is all we can muster against Garden City, Kansas, in a 10–1 loss. With two more losses, Williston becomes a debacle as we finish 0–5 in the tournament. Once again, little things kept killing us. Missed signs, missing the cut off man from the outfield costing extra bases, not sliding allowing for a tag standing up all contribute to our failures. Looking at the scores, we really only received one good outing from our pitchers. Baseball discipline is nowhere to be seen.

Listen to Brian D. recall a moment after a poorly played game, "Helbs went on an epic rant in the hotel room. I think he dropped forty-three f-bombs in two minutes. Later, he gets a call from the hotel manager telling him the boys were being really loud and using foul language, and asked him if he could get us to calm down because there was a person next door that was in hospice care dying of cancer." Somewhere, somehow, things have got to change. After the final loss in North Dakota, we are scheduled for a doubleheader against the Billings teams. So backtracking on the road to Williston, we head back to Billings. The players are subdued, and they should be. I have little to say because I'm trying to find the right words.

We have arrived in Billings and find our motel on North 27th Street, two blocks from Cobb Field, where we will play. In the morning, Coach Mike finds me sitting on the grass in front of the motel just staring straight ahead in total concentration. He told me later that he didn't want to bother me because he knew I was in deep thought, and he was right. The team has been quiet all day, so I know they have been in concentration in their own way. Before the game, I say a few words, but that is all. Game time against the Royals is five o'clock. Jeff is our pitcher, and he throws two innings, Troy throws two innings, and Greg R. throws one, and the Cards explode for thirteen runs on fourteen hits for a 13–1 whitewash. Wow! Troy also picked up three runs batted in. The second game, versus the Billings Scarlets, saw Lawson R. and Greg R. team up on the mound for a 7–3 win. Chris H. S.'s two-run home run in the seventh sealed the deal. The most impressive statistic of the day was that the Cards played errorless baseball the entire night. I know it wasn't anything I said. I guess the players had a little meeting of their own. Time to head to Rapid City. Our caravan heads east on I-90 out of Billings, to Buffalo, Wyoming, and on through Gillette and Spearfish, South Dakota, to Rapid City.

In our first game, on June 29, on a windy, cloudy day, Rob has a great day with a triple, home run, three hits, four RBIs, and three runs scored at the leadoff spot against Colorado Springs. His three-run home run breaks up a 6–6 tie in extra innings. Brian D. also picks up three hits, and he is the winning pitcher, in relief in the seventh, for a 10–6 win. Big inning woes haunt us again against El Segundo the following day as Jeff, Greg, and Dave struggle, allowing four in the first and six in the second, and we "can't hang," 12–4. We have become hot and cold! Now we are cold, losing 9–1 to Rapid City, after I have a neat radio/TV interview on the local channel. Oops! We are hot again as Jeff goes all the way in a 9–1, fourteen-hit barrage against Las Vegas Durango. Then Greg S. throws a three-hit shutout against Boulder, Colorado, and Troy and Brian D shut down Burnsville, Minnesota, 9–3. But in the next game versus Boulder, on the Fourth of July, in the Firecracker Tournament, they score twice in the bottom of the sixth to go ahead 5–4, and that is how it ended. Bang! However, I feel much better after Rapid City than I felt after Williston. What will we find in Miles City?

Miles City has become like home on the road! We are always welcome, and the town folks seem to be glad we are back. Ephrata, Washington, is our first opponent in MC (that has become the affectionate name for Miles City). Greg S. earns his sixth victory in a two hitter, 3–1. This game has given us one sure constant. Earlier in this season, Rob C. put together a string of seventeen straight games without an error. After this game, he finished another string of perfect defense with his fifteenth straight errorless game. He plays second base for us, beside Bill W., giving us a great middle infield. Plenty of time is spent talking about hitting and pitching, but not enough time on defense. Rob has given me something to talk about. Jeff P. gets the start, in the next outing, against ol' nemesis, the Eugene Pepsi-Challengers. He pitches well enough but doesn't get the offensive support, and we succumb, 5–3. Rapid City is next. Nick A. is a surprise starter. He has really struggled this season and comes in with an 0–4 record and over 11.00 era. The Cards stand up for him, getting seven runs on ten hits, and Nick picks up his first win of the season with a 7–3 victory. Greg R. finishes the game on the mound for a save. Tonight, we can hang! Brian D. will tackle the MC Mavericks in tomorrow's game. He goes all the way, and the Cards win 4–2.

The Yellowstone River runs through Miles City, as well as the smaller tributary river called the Tongue. Both Rivers are an attraction, although the Yellowstone is much larger. Players have found safe places to have fun in the rivers, helped out by the locals. One young local, and a fan of the Cardinals, has taken it upon himself, with encouragement of some players, to show them some good fishing holes. They would follow him on his bike to the "good" spots. His name was Tony T. At games, Tony would be our bat boy, and that is where the fishermen would make arrangements with him to meet, when we were not playing. You will hear more from Tony in a few years.

It's Saturday, and we have two games to play to get to the championship. First is Eugene, Oregon, again. They had beaten us earlier, so it should be a tough game, but with Greg S. on the mound, he held them to four hits and picked up his seventh win in a 3–1 game. Chris C. had two hits, his second a two-run single to break the tie. Coach Mike and I had a discussion as to whether we should pitch Greg in the first game or hold him to the second. Obviously, the thought was, "Go for the now." I should report that I was ejected in the seventh inning arguing an interference call against our base runner, Rob. Another case of "I was right, ump was wrong, ump wins!" Anyway, we have to get ready for Rapid City. Winner plays Sunday for the championship. Jeff P. is hit pretty hard in four innings. Nick A., Greg R., and Lawson can't do much better. We lose, 11–7. We will be back in 1995, but for now we still have a little bit of business to take care of. The Cards will end this road trip in Cody, Wyoming, and in Yellowstone.

Headed to Cody, we have a busy schedule for the next two days. We've got a game scheduled with Cody, a whitewater trip on the Shoshone River, and a ride through Yellowstone National Park. The Cardinals leave Billings, going west on I-90 until they get to Laurel, where they turn south on US 212, another short drive to a junction at Rockvale, where they pick up US 310 to south of Bridger and Montana 72. At the Wyoming border, it becomes Wyoming 120 to Cody. Been here before, but many of my players haven't. They were fascinated about the guy who drives around in his fancy Cadillac with a wide spread of Texas Longhorn bull horns attached to the front. After a short break and something to eat, we get ready for the game. Greg R. gets the start, followed by Troy, and Chris H. S. Nineteen hits and eighteen runs later, we finish the game 18–4. Rob has turned in a six-for-six game, scoring five runs, and driving in three. Lawson has one of his best days with two hits and three RBIs. That's the final game of the road trip. Our record on the road this year is 11–10.

The Shoshone River is next, followed by Yellowstone. The Cardinals are scheduled for a whitewater trip on the Shoshone River outside of Cody. It is mid-July. As I've said before, experiences on whitewater trips depend on weather and time of year. We hit a bad time. The river was low and rapids small, so the excitement was varied. The water was wet and warm. It was nothing like the experiences I've had on the Snake, Gallitan, Yellowstone rivers. But it was worth it. A short trip into Yellowstone is on the menu. The Cards enter Yellowstone from the east side out of Wapiti, Wyoming. A Wapiti is an elk, and this part of the country is abundant with elk, thus the town's name. The Cards will take the circle route around the lake to West Thumb, then to Old Faithful, and the Grand Canyon of Yellowstone with a view of the falls. This is where we take our team picture. It's time to head home. So from the Canyon, we head up US89 through Paradise Valley to Livingston, Montana. Here, we pick up I-90 and head east to Billings. We flew into Billings, we will fly out of Billings. We have four more conference games to play.

Greg S. picks up his eighth win with no losses in an 11–3 victory, with offensive help on a Bill W. home run. Jeff shuts out Pasadena at home two days later. Chris C. is three for four with three RBIs and a triple. On three days' rest, Greg throws six innings and Brian D. closes in a tight 3–2 win over La Verne. Bill W.'s two-run double in the third puts Cards up. To finish the four-game sweep, Troy goes all the way in the second game of the day, at home for a 5–1 victory.

All five runs are scored in the bottom of the sixth to turn the game around. Mike J.'s triple led the hitting in the sixth. The Cards head to District Playoffs. Facing Covina, in the opener at Claremont

High School, Greg S. and Covina's pitcher tangle in a classic dual with the score tied 1–1 going into the bottom of the ninth inning. On a 2–0 pitch, Chris H. S. leads off with a home run to left field where it is marked 356 feet from home plate. Cards win an exciting opener and have their fifth straight win. In game 2 of districts, Jeff P. steps up and strikes out eleven while walking only one and holds Arcadia to one run for the Cards sixth straight win. Adrian S. had four hits, and Brian D. had three of the Cards' fifteen-hit parade. Greg S. gets tied up in another duel, but this time, Arcadia, on a home run in the eighth, the Cards lose 4–3. Claremont loses the final game of the season, 11–5, and are eliminated. What an up-and-down year. Rob leads the team in hitting with a .390 average. He had 52 runs scored. Bill W. hit 343. But the most impressive statistic was the combination of our middle infield with Bill at short and Rob at second. Both players, in very busy positions, made only six errors each. Rob had a .969 fielding average, and Bill had a .967 fielding average. After all was said, the Williston Tournament was an awakening for the Cards, as they played very good defense, hit the ball well, and in crucial moments, got some great pitching.

SHENANIGANS

In 1980, this road trip started as a one-time adventure. It's 1995, and I can't believe that this will be the sixteenth season that the Cardinals will travel. It has become a traditional yearly event, and most players have come to expect it. The Cardinals have traveled all over the great northwest, appearing in towns some players had never heard of, but got the opportunity to experience. Cody, Casper, Sheridan, Wyoming; Lethbridge, Medicine Hat, Calgary, Canada; Mandan, Bismarck, Williston, Minot, North Dakota; Miles City, Billings, Great Falls, Montana; Belle Fourche, Deadwood, Rapid City, South Dakota; Yellowstone, Glacier, Mount Rushmore, Little Big Horn, and other National Parks or Monuments; the Snake River, Gallatin River, Yellowstone River, Shoshone River, Missouri River, and Bow River are just some places that the Cards have been. This year, I will visit some of the same places again, but for many players, it will be new to them. Win or lose, when we get home, the feeling has always been that this was fun. Obviously, that's what makes it worth doing it again.

For several years now, the Cards have opened the season in a tournament in Ontario, California. They will do it again this season. However, before the Ontario tournament, on May 23, the season will open in Pasadena in a conference game, with returner Greg S. on the mound. He continues doing his thing, winning ball games, with a 7–2 win, with help from Brian D. in relief. The Cards picked up fourteen hits, all singles.

The next evening, Claremont faced Damien, a team from their school in La Verne. During pregame infield workouts, our catcher Doug B. is injured in the hand trying to stop an errant throw. He will be out four to six weeks. Jeff W., new to the Cards this year, can't hold them in a 5–3 loss. Cedric, another new player, is called upon to do the catching duties. I tried to have this game rescheduled because it conflicted with the annual high school baseball all-star game, but was denied. The all-star game was being held in Rancho Cucamonga at the Epicenter, a minor league ballpark for the Dodgers. Rob C., Darren W., Doug, and myself had to leave the game in the third inning for the all-star game. I had been selected to coach in that game as well as our three players. As far as the Ontario Tournament, we played well and hit the ball well, and in a game against Etiwanda, the Cards won the tournament with a 14–7 victory. James S., another new player for us, pitched, with help from J.J.M. Once again Cedric caught, with Doug calling the pitches.

By the time we are ready to cast off into the wild northwest, we are 11–6. There have been some interesting games besides the Ontario tournament. Against La Verne, Andre S. pitches six strong innings and leaves the game with a 7–1 lead. Jeff, Troy, Brian cannot hang on to the lead for three innings, and the Cards drop a tough game to La Verne, on a cold breezy day. Five days later, after the weather warms up, finally, Las Vegas rolls into town for a two-game set. Greg S. holds them to a 4–4 tie, but Greg R. allows a run in the last inning and Claremont drops the opener, 5–4. In the second game of the double-dip, a double by Rob C., in the sixth, scores Rich D., who had walked and stole second, to give the Cards a split, 7–6. Two tough games.

Ten days before we leave, we play La Verne again, with Greg S. on the mound. He is off his game, walking five and allowing six runs in four innings. Jeff picks up on the mound for three plus innings, and J. J. gets the save in a wild 16–10 game, on the hottest day of the year, so far. Rob had four RBIs, Mike J. was 2–4, with a double and three RBIs. Dave R. had taken over duties as our catcher until Doug could return, which will happen during the road trip. This win marked the 700th win for the Cardinals (700–363). A good send-off for our upcoming road trip.

So here we are again in Lethbridge. Their coach, Scott O, and I have established a good relationship ever since our first meeting in Santa Maria eighteen years ago. We fly into Great Falls, and drive up to Lethbridge on I-15, a well-traveled road for us. Once again, the Cards enter Canada at Sweetgrass, and on the Alberta side, a town called Coutts. Just north of Coutts is a large elk ranch, which is something new to our Southern California men. Some take pictures, because that day, the elk were close to the road. Traveling up Alberta 4, the Cards cross the Milk River at the town with the same name. The Milk is a 729-mile river that begins out of the Rocky Mountains in Montana and flows northeast into Alberta. It then takes a turn to the south and flows back into Montana, where it will eventually meet the Missouri River, near Fort Peck.

Our first opponent in the tournament is Great Falls. We score eight runs on eight hits, and Greg S. picks up his fourth victory. The Cards will stay at the same motel that they have been staying at each year, across from the ballpark. J. J. gets the call against a new foe, a team from Seattle, Washington. He turns in a complete game, 6–1. In the second game of the day, Andre struggles against Medicine Hat, Alberta, and takes a loss, 7–6. Claremont gets back to winning ways with a 6–3 win, spun by Greg R. with help from Jeff and Brian D. It was an early game, so the Cardinals are scheduled for a team picnic down by the Saskatchewan River. Hamburgers, hot dogs, and all the fixin's make for a fun team get together. Camp cook Brian D. is in charge. As if, a baseball game is not enough, a whiffle ball game is organized. It's an all-around good day.

I have found, while visiting Lethbridge, on several occasions, that Alberta girls are somehow attracted to California boys! It's happened again. One late night—tell me if you've heard this story before—I

get a call from the front desk. They tell me that a mother is calling, looking for her daughter, who is supposed to be visiting with a
Claremont player. What's his name? Cedric. Okay, so I go to Cedric's
room and knock on the door. He answers and appears to have just
been awakened. I ask him about his potential visitor. No, she is not
here, so I wander around the room realizing that no other player is in
the room, but I also notice that the bathroom door is shut. Hmmm!
This must be déjà vu. The sleuth in me says, *Open the bathroom door.*
Surprise! Once again, a girl is in there! "Your mom wants you home."
She is embarrassed and leaves. We are in Canada, so that's a $13 fine,
Canadian, and one-day suspension for Cedric.

A 10–4 victory over hometown Lethbridge puts us into tomorrow's championship game, against Lethbridge, again. Greg S. is on the
hill. Several mistakes early in the game puts us behind 8–2 after five
innings—the most runs Greg S. has ever allowed for us. Five singles,
a walk, a forced out, and a sacrifice fly score three runs in the sixth.
Dave opens the eighth inning with a home run down the left field
line. Troy's single later in the inning scores Brian D. with the winning
run, 9–8. J. J. pitched two scoreless innings to save it for Greg S. James
was 4–4 at the plate, as Brian D. kept preaching, "No! we won't lose,
we won't lose!" Cards wind up with seventeen hits. Cedric keeps score!
Claremont wins the Lethbridge Tournament. Headed back into our
homeland, we will make a stop in Great Falls.

In a lackluster performance, the Cardinals drop one to Great
Falls, 6–4. There is really nothing exciting to report. Rapid City
should generate much more enthusiasm. It does! In the first game,
Colorado Springs absorbs an eighteen-hit barrage, and the Cards score
nineteen runs for a shortened 19–3 win. Troy has three hits and four
RBIs. Dave hits a home run leading off the fifth, Darren has three hits
and scores four times. Greg S. picks up his sixth win. In game 2, J. J.
gives up three runs in the second, and six runs in the third, and the
Cardinals go quietly 12–2. For the Cards, the tournament continues
like this, hot one day, cold the next. Against Burnsville, Minnesota,
the Cards completed a weird feat. They scored sixteen runs on eight

hits, eight walks, and eight Burnsville errors, all in just five innings. Ugly! And time consuming. James was the benefactor on the mound.

One day, just as we were to leave for a game, Cedric E. informs me that he is sick. He looks sick. I told him to stay back in his room and rest while we go to the game. Get something to eat. He says okay. We go to the game and return. I check with him, and he says he feels better.

"Did you get anything to eat?"

"Yes."

Great. I go to my room, and everything is quiet. Now, I know I have told you that the Rapid City tournament is the Firecracker Tournament, so what should you expect? I'm lying on the bed watching TV, and all of a sudden, *bang!* Someone has lit a firecracker. If you have stayed in northern motels, you know that the rooms are connected by hallways indoors. I go outside my room and look around and don't see anyone, so I walk down the hallway and around a corner. There in front of one of our rooms is a bowl with firecracker residue in it. I go into the room and ask Adrian if he knows anything about it. He says no, only that it went off, he doesn't know who lit it. Okay, I pick up the bowl and realize that it is from the motel restaurant. OMG! (That expression hadn't been developed yet.) So I'm knocking on Cedric's door. He answers again, like he has been sleeping.

"Cedric, what did you have for lunch?"

"Some soup."

"Cedric, is this the bowl you had soup in?" (What a sleuth).

"Um, um, yes."

"See me in the morning, and we will talk about this then."

Cedric knocks on my door the next morning. I let him in, and we discuss the shenanigans that he has been involved in while on this road trip. He can't deny anything. I thought about it overnight, and I told Cedric to pack his bags, he's going home. He can tell his parents anything he wants as to why he's coming home. That late afternoon, around 5:30 p.m., I drive Cedric to the bus station. I put seventeen-year-old Cedric on a Jackrabbit Lines from Rapid City to

Billings, where he will catch a Trailways to Claremont. He should arrive by 5:30 a.m., thirty-six hours later. He has become the first player I have ever sent home. Stick around, this story ends well.

The Cards fall into a funk! They lose four straight games in Rapid City, committing fifteen errors and striking out thirty-five times. Not a good showing as they prepare to leave for MC. Before we take off, I go to the front desk to take care of the bill. I'm told that we have a $1,000 phone bill. What, how can that be? There was no cell phones in those days, so players who wanted to call home had to use the phones in their rooms, but to call out of your room, you had to dial 90 first. The area code on most of the calls was 909, which made these calls home confusing on the bill. The 90 was the number of a foreign country. I went to each room and collected all the phone numbers that had been called and took them to the desk, where we matched them with the massive bill. They matched. After making a call to the phone company and matching area codes, they were able to amend the problem and the bill. This mix-up seemed to match the mix-up we were having on the field. On to Miles City.

It's the Fourth of July, and we are headed out of Rapid City on our way to Miles City. The quickest way there is to take I-90 to Spearfish and transcend onto SD 34 to Belle Fourche and pick up US 212 west, toward MC. We will cross into Wyoming for about twenty miles until we reach Montana, near Alzada, on the Little Missouri River. It is sixty-three miles to Broadus, where we will cross the Powder River and make a change onto Montana highway 59. Seventy-six miles to our destination, somewhere on the road from Broadus, I decide to pull over and allow the players to have their own Fourth of July firework show. It is nighttime, and we are in the middle of nowhere, so it should be safe. They had a good time dodging bottle rockets, lighting firecrackers, and other fireworks. I felt it would be better to give them a chance to light their fireworks here, rather than in town. It worked out fine. The Cards will be "home" soon.

Our first game in Miles City is against Las Vegas Knights. Not much has changed from Rapid City. Four more errors, only three hits, and ten more strikeouts and we are shut down, 6–0. This string of poor playing and a lack of hitting calls for a special workout right after the game, so the Cards meet on Tedesco field, right behind Denton, for a special session. It seemed to have an effect.

The next day, the Cardinals play another California team, from Lafayette. The Cards had played them once before, in the 1988 state playoffs, and had won 15–4. In this game, Greg S. started for us, and Brian D., finished a 6–4 victory. Dave hit a three-run home run, in the first, to get us going. Mandan, North Dakota, is our next opponent. Somebody woke up! Every player in the starting lineup had a hit, including Rob, who was three for five, a double and triple and three RBIs. Dave had two hits and three RBIs and another home run. Adrian had three hits. J. J. collected a hit, and went all the way on the mound as we won our second straight game, 15–0. Jeff W. starts the next game, and Greg R. finishes as the Cards get another shutout, 11–0. This time over Miles City. Troy's two-run home run gets us going in this one, and Dave's third home run in three days, caps off the scoring.

There is not a lot to do off the field in Miles City. The biggest attraction is to go back to the ballpark and watch another team play, or just talk to the fans, who seem always interested in our California players. However, there is another activity that the players have created themselves. The Buckboard Inn is situated right off of the interstate (in California, we call them freeways). Every town in Montana, it seems, has a combination gas station, mini mart, casino, called the Town Pump. The casino was always a popular place. But the Claremont players have invented the "Town Pump Challenge." Here are the rules of the challenge, as explained by Justin B. From the Town Pump, get two sixty-four-ounce cups filled with dark soda—Coke or Pepsi or Dr. Pepper. You must have a small layer of ice, no higher than the first line on the cup. The challenge is to drink both cups in fifteen minutes. Get ready, get set, go! Here is Brian D.'s description of his challenge: "It took me five minutes to get through one and one half cups, and I couldn't touch the rest of it. And I have never thrown up more in my life!" A local player, Shawn Mc., reported, "I wasn't dumb enough to try it, but was happy to help anyone willing enough to give it a go." It is good to see our players sharing their experiences with other players from other teams, especially the Miles City boys.

We have to finish the real tournament. Andre battles El Segundo but falls short, 4–3. Despite that loss, we have reached the semis on Saturday. In the early game, it'll be a rematch with Lafayette and a rematch for Greg S. He will pick up his seventh win, and Brian D. will make his fifth save, and the Cardinals will win, 6–5. Three RBIs by Rob and two from Dave are the big sticks of the day. In game 2 of the day, Troy doesn't share the same support, as the Cards can only muster three hits and one run to finish the tournament with a 5–1 loss. Dave and Adrian are selected to the All-Tournament team. In the tournament, Dave hit home runs in three consecutive games. On the road, this year, Claremont is 12–10. Not spectacular.

The Cardinals have seven more games to play before the playoffs begin. In the first game back, the team is on the road at Damien, with Jeff W. on the mound. He does a great job in a shortened game because of a ten-run rule, 13–2. Home runs by James, Dave, and Brian D. give him all the support he needs. Let's talk about Brian's home run. Earlier in the year, at school where he attends and I teach, I made a $50 bet with him, one day, that I could swim a mile in our school pool. I spent three weeks at lunchtime in the pool getting ready. Finally, the day comes for the action to happen. He has gathered several friends and teammates to watch. It will take seventy-five laps in the pool for a mile, and I pace myself. Finally, with just one lap to go, I decide to sprint, and cramped up halfway to the end. I dog-paddled the final distance and won my bet. Well, I'm not going to collect, so I gave Brian a chance to win his money back by telling him that if he hits a home run this summer, we'd be even. When he hit his home run at Damien, before he gets to first, he turns and points at me. He remembered. I thought that it was cool. The Cardinals finish the rest of the regular season with four more victories, and they will enter the District Playoffs. In a 4–1 victory, over La Verne, Doug returns from injury and gets two hits and three RBIs.

In Districts, Greg S. opens with 15–6 win, picking up his ninth win, getting help from Brian D. on the mound. We drop one to Arcadia despite thirteen hits, bounce back on Dave's seventh home run and defeat Pasadena, 15–5. We move on to Area playoffs, a few days later, and Greg S. picks up his tenth and last win of the season over Ventura, 5–3. It is Greg's twenty-eighth win of his Cardinal career, and sets the record for most wins in the Cards uniform. Camarillo shuts us out 10–0, Troy outduels Arcadia before Greg S. loses, 9–5, to Camarillo in a rematch. The loss marks the end of the season and the end of the line for Greg, Brian D., Rob, Darren, Doug, Rich, and Dave.

Dave and Greg S. are voted co-Most Valuable Players by the team.

DEAD MAN'S PASS

In January of 1996, Cedric E. comes into my office at the high school and wants to talk to me. He tells me he wants to play this summer on the Legion team and go on the road trip. Remember, I sent Cedric home in July last year. We had a good talk. I told him that he'd have to be a leader and help make sure the newbies knew what was expected of them. He could show some of this leadership during the high school baseball season. He said he would. I learned years ago to never say, "You'll never play for me again!" That's because, working with young men and women, one year can make a big difference in maturity. Cedric is a great example of this philosophy, and trust.

The year 1996 actually marks the twenty-fifth season of the Claremont Cardinals. 1972 was our first year and 1980 our first road trip. The early season tournament in Ontario will give us a good look at what we have for this season. In the first game, against a league opponent, we get three hits and no runs. We played well, and the pitching of first-year pitcher, Andrew P., was very encouraging. Despite the lack of offense, I had a positive feeling. However, it took us four more games before we achieved our first win. In our fourth game of the year, Jeff

W. hits two bombs and drives in five runs, but it is not enough. We are getting good pitching but are struggling at the plate. Mike J. and Cedric have a three-RBI game for our sixth win, against Pasadena. Andy P. and Jeff W. follow up with home runs in a fourteen-run game against Damien. But once again, we are not consistent. The Cards head north with six wins, nine losses, and one suspended game.

From Ontario, Billings is our destination once more. This year, the Cards open up the road in Medicine Hat, Alberta, so from Billings, they travel north on US 87 to Grass Range, Montana, and pick up US 191 until they reach Montana 66. (Remember these directions, because I won't). That will take them to US 2, then west to Havre. From Havre, the route takes us north to the Canadian border at Wild Horse, then on to Medicine Hat. Road weary, the Cards drop the game to the Medicine Hat Moose Monarchs, 13–5. In the fourth inning after getting a hit, Cedric slides into second and somehow breaks his thumb. What a sad piece of luck. Cedric will stay with the team for the remainder of the trip and be a leader, doing the necessary little team jobs.

The following day, the Cardinals head to Lethbridge for their tournament. In the first two games, we've scored one run and get ready to play Lethbridge. The *Lethbridge Herald* called us "listless losers." Well, they were right. After being picked to win the tournament, we had ho-hummed our way through the first two games. On this day, we had a picnic, played some whiffle ball, and decided, as a team, that we had to show some "intestinal fortitude!" (there is another way of putting it). In the game, we did just that! The game started at 8:00 p.m., but that didn't make it a night game. We are so far north that it will be light until 11:30 p.m. On the mound, Andy P. over powered the Elks for six innings, striking out ten. Troy K. finished the game and picked up a save, as Cards win, 5–3. Andy P. had a big two-run single in the sixth, and Troy, and Danny R. each had two hits. The Cards were neither listless nor losers! Then the rains came.

Lethbridge officials had prepared for the rains. Henderson Field was washed out, but thirty kilometers down the road, in a small town called Picture Butte, there is another field that was readied for play. So at 1:30, we met the Spokane Royals. The Cards had built up a 10–2 lead in the fifth inning. Joe H. had hit a home run and was up again in the sixth when he hit another high drive to left field. The fences were chain length with no protective plastic covering, and the left fielder went up high to try to catch the ball. When he came down, he had impaled himself on the fence. I thought he hung himself! The game was halted as they waited for an ambulance. The delay was about forty-five minutes. Joe's second home run made the score 14–2, and the officials decided, wisely, to end the game at this point, with the Cards having a victory. Joe was three for four with five RBIs and three runs scored. A later report from the hospital says the Spokane player will be all right. The Cards will face Medicine Hat once again in the tournament. This time, they take care of the Moose-Monarchs, 10–6, as James S. slugs another home run. We are done with Lethbridge, Picture Butte, and the *Lethbridge Herald!*

Personally, I look forward to every road trip all year long. But with this one, I was really excited because I had scheduled some more Canadian activities. We will leave Lethbridge and head to Lake Louise in the Banff National Park. This area is beautiful, and I had taken the team there a few years ago. We head north up Alberta 2, 168 kilometers to Calgary, where we find Trans-Canada 1, west, toward the Park. The Cards will stay overnight, actually three nights, at a small motel in a place called Dead Man's Pass. The motel is a 1950s'-style setting with small cottages scattered around the grounds, all separated from one another. It is very quaint, right below a mountain range called The Three Sisters. (I know I've mentioned the Sisters before.)

The next day, we take the road into the park and to Lake Louise. The players spend the day wandering around the area, taking pictures of the lake, the chalet, themselves and everything around. Horseback riding was an option. I have had the players prepare to bring their uniforms, because we will take our team picture at the lake. At the close of the trip to Lake Louise, we head back to Dead Man's Pass. That evening, I take volunteers, most of the players, into Calgary. I drop the eighteen-year-old players off at the French Maiden, a bar and grill for adults. In Canada, this was all legal. For the younger players, I take them to an amusement park. On the way, in the bus, Eddie J. spots two young ladies on the street and shouts out of the bus a pickup line. They shout back, "Come back in three years, little boy!" It was hilarious! After a few hours, we head back to Dead Man's Pass. The Cards have one more activity in Canada. In the morning, the team drives east, a short way to a little town called Kananaskis. Here, the Cards have scheduled a whitewater trip on the Bow River. The Bow River originates out of a glacier in the Canadian Rockies and flows eastward, joining the South Saskatchewan River, which eventually will empty into the Hudson Bay, in the east. The water is great for rapids, but, obviously, it is cold. Add the Bow River to the Cardinals' river excursions. One more night in Canada at "The Pass" and Claremont will be on its way, south to Billings for another tournament.

J. J. throws six strong innings in the opener versus Boise, Idaho, as Cards open up with a 6–2 win. Jeff W. has a two-run home run at Cobb Field. Our second game is at a different field, up the road and across the street from MSUB, Urbaska Field—no sunflower seeds, please. Andy P. and Troy K. allow two runs and four hits to Aurora, Colorado, and Claremont makes it 2–0. After dropping two straight, all at Urbaska, we are back at Cobb Field. Troy has a hot day against Medicine Hat with two doubles, a home run, and five runs batted in, in a 10–6 win. We split six games in Billings, so we look ahead to Miles City. Troy was named to the all-tourney team.

In MC, Hancock, Michigan, is our first opponent, and Andy D. will pitch. He is the benefactor of twelve runs and thirteen hits to pick up the win, 12–6. After losing a game on the Fourth of July to Dallas, Texas, the Cards go back to the Buckboard to clean up and then head back to the ballpark for the fireworks. They start somewhere around 10:00 p.m., because it is still light in Montana. The next evening, we pack the stands for the Miles City game. Ben D., batting ninth, homers in the third to tie the game, 1–1. The town folk have always rooted for us, except when we play their team. It is a good show for the fans, and after the top of the sixth, the Cards lead 3–1. Then the rains came, and out comes the tarp. The rain delay will last over an hour, so during that time, I decide to entertain the fans with a song. Standing out in the rain near home plate, I start singing, "It ain't a gonna rain no more, more, it ain't a gonna rain no more," six stanzas! One thing I like about Miles City is that they will do everything they can to complete the games. Earlier, I have seen them use flame blowers, large fans, etc., to prepare the field. This year, they have a tarp. After a little over an hour, we are ready to finish the game. In the top of the seventh, Miles City gets sloppy with three errors, and on Jeff W.'s double, the Cardinals pick up two runs for a 5–1 win. Andy P. has struck out fourteen and allowed two hits. James S. will be on the mound to face, for the first time, the Kennewick, Washington Dusters. We give up seven runs on six hits, commit four errors, and lose, 7–2. In reverse the next day, Andre goes all the way, and we defeat a team from Eden Prairie, Minnesota, 11–4. That puts us into the semifinals against Kennewick. Troy and Henry C. can't handle them, and it's over for us on the road this season. Danny hit .647, and J. J. hit .500 in the tournament and are chosen for the all-tournament team. We were 9–9 on the road.

Our first game back home, was at Pasadena. It went eleven innings and was called because of darkness, 3–3. Andrew and James pitch well. We play the same team the next day, and on a J. J. home run, we outscore Pasadena 10–9. J. J. gets a complete game victory over West Covina, but after that, we finish the season like we started it, with a four-game losing streak. Troy was voted our team MVP.

THE FOURTH ON THE COLUMBIA

The year 1997 was another turnaround year for the Cards. We won sixteen games on the field, and our team earned run average was 7.95, so it was a tough season for us. To begin, we split the first two games of the season. In the third game, against Montclair, an odd thing happened. With Montclair up in the second inning, their first five hitters did not record an official at bat. Jared M. was our pitcher, and he walked the first batter, hit the second with a pitch, gave up a sacrifice bunt, and walked the next two hitters before a double play helped him out (walks, hit by pitch, sacrifices all count as plate appearances, but do not count as official at bats when determining batting averages). We lost that game, 11–2. In the ninth game of the season, Andrew P. struck out sixteen and walked seven, but went all the way in a nine-inning game and threw a no-hitter. Claremont Cardinals' first ever nine-inning no-hitter. It took 166 pitches. Later, just before we left, Josh threw a two-hit shutout. Following the shutout by Josh, the Cards get wrapped up in the wildest game they have ever played, facing West Covina at home. A total of 39 hits, 19 walks, six errors, and 29 stolen bases—no one was thrown out—contribute to the highest total scoring game, for the Cards. Tom O. led the way with four hits and four runs batted in. Joe H. had four RBIs on three hits. West Covina hit the only home run of the game, and after all the action in the first 8 1/2 innings, it was Tim C. laying down a squeeze bunt to score Justin B. with the winning run, 22–21. Against Damien, we had given up twenty-one runs, so it was either "eat or be eaten." We will head to Cody, Wyoming, with at 10–11 record.

On June 23, the Cardinals climb aboard a Delta flight to Salt Lake City once again. That's where they will make their connection to Billings. It's been done several times. After they land in Billings, they will pick up their rental vehicles and drive to Cody, Wyoming. When you say Cody, you have to think Yellowstone. The Cards have done this several times, going north and going south. We have two games in Cody, but my plan is to try to save my pitching for the Billings tournament. We stayed at the Rainbow Park Motel.

In the first game, Eddie J. starts on the mound. Eddie is an infielder, and currently he has been playing first base. We collect twelve hits but only two runs, and Cody beats us, 10–2. In the second game, I throw Jared M., Tim O., and Cliff G., and they manage to keep the score down as we win, 4–3. Claremont leaves Cody the next morning and heads to Yellowstone National Park. Once again with a new crew, we will tour the park. We wind up in Gardner, at the north end of Yellowstone, where I have made reservations at the Westernaire Motel. In the morning, we gear up with our whitewater gear and take a ride on the rapids of the Yellowstone River, through Yankee Jim Canyon and beyond. Once again, after the whitewater trip, we head to "The Corral" for buffalo burgers and shakes. The Cards then head back up to Billings to begin their tournament there. Tim, Jared, Cliff, are unable to stop a new opponent, the Columbia Basin River Dogs, out of Pasco, Washington, 16–1. After another tough loss, Pete B. tosses a nifty five hitter against Pocatello, Idaho, and we get a victory, 6–1. Two more losses and we have two days to get to Kennewick, Washington, for a tournament there over July Fourth. From Billings, it's I-90 west, 226 miles to Butte, where we will stay for the night at the Comfort Inn. I find a place uptown where the players can have a good meal, and it's on me. The next day, we leave as soon as we can get all the players awake and loaded on the vans. We have another 345 miles to go. I don't know who scheduled this, but he should be shot! So it's I-90 through Idaho and into Washington. The Cards will make a pit stop in the small town of Ritzville. Out of Ritzville, we leave the interstate and pick up US 395, south. I have designated a check in point at an exit on the road, so that we stay together in our caravan, near Connell. Myself and Coach Brian pull out and wait for the last vehicle. It doesn't come for thirty minutes. Uh-oh. I get into my van and head back down the road, and shortly, I spot our third car racing to get to the off ramp. I turn around. When I get back, Eddie, who was driving, tells me he fell asleep behind the wheel and they ran off the road! That's not good. Eddie is a player, but our situation right now is that we are missing one coach, so a player has to drive one of the vehicles. Anyway, we finally make it to Kennewick on the Columbia River. We have crossed the Snake River, which flows into the Columbia right near Kennewick. This was the longest drive between destinations that I have scheduled. There is a longer one waiting for us after Kennewick. Before we left, I instructed the players to eat some fruit on the road rather than the "junk" they usually buy when we make a stop. Some did, some didn't. Tom didn't.

Our hotel, The Red Lion Inn, is right on the Columbia River. You could jump out of my window into the river. The Cards have a game coming up, but before the game, Tom comes to me with a problem. He can't poop! He hasn't pooped in two days! He is constipated! I find a store, buy some Metamucil, make him take it, and tell him to stay in his room while we go to the game. Pete is on the mound for us and gets plenty of support as the Cards pick up nineteen hits and twelve runs against Boise, Idaho. Garret O., Andy, and Eddie each have three hits. When I got back to the hotel from the game, I went to Tom's room. He was on the pot! Hallelujah!

For the season, I have had two young coaches help me. They both played on the Claremont Cardinals, so they know what to expect, which is good. Brian D. and Darren W. recently played and were great team leaders. However, Darren has not been with us because he has had to remain at home for a week, so the arrangements were that I would pick him up while in Kennewick. I bought a plane ticket to Spokane, Washington, on Southwest Airlines from Ontario for him and drove to Spokane to pick him up. I also had made arrangements for a rental of a seventeen-people pontoon boat and two Jet Skis for the rest of the day and evening on the Columbia River. After our 9:00 a.m. game against Bend, Oregon, of which we squeaked by 7–6, we left to pick up the boat and Jet Skis. The players spent the rest of the day on the river and had a blast. Two at a time on the Jet Skis. The Coast Guard checked us once to make sure we had seventeen life jackets. We had. We watched the fireworks show, which was in the middle of the river, from our boat. It turned out, at night, the boat had no working lights and became a hazard on the river. Justin B. reports, "The night our pontoon boat almost sank because our lights stopped working and boats were buzzing by us because they didn't see us, and we started to take on water."

Coach Brian says, "I just remember I'm in the front of the pontoon when the waves came rolling in, and we started to teeter forward and me yelling at everyone to run back and level it out! I thought we were going to capsize!"

After bailing some water, they got the boat back to the dock, with helpful wake speeds. That just made the whole adventure more fun.

The following day, we had a game scheduled with the host team, Kennewick, at 3:00 p.m. The players and coaches got a chance to sleep in a little. At about 1:30 p.m., in the coaches' room, we are getting ready to head to the ballpark. At that moment, for some reason, Coach Brian and I met eye to eye—literally. That's where we both stopped and continued to stare at each other. It became a staring contest, and it lasted a long time. Both Coach and I maintained composure, and soon several players gathered around to watch. We could have sold tickets. At some time, someone mentioned that we had to go to the game. I knew that, but I'm not losing! Finally, we all started to get antsy, and without a smile, and with the authority of a head coach, I said, "We gotta go." Brian agreed, and we declared the contest a tie. With James going all the way, we lost the game, 7–4. The Cardinals showing in Kennewick was not very impressive, as we lost the final game against the River Dogs, 9–2, despite a home run from Andy P.

The hotel on the river was a really nice place, but we have two days to get to Miles City, which is 146 miles farther than Billings from Kennewick. Speaking of "on the road again," we just can't wait to get on the road again, gotta leave early in the morning. This Fourth of July was fun despite the lack of success on the field, and the players were upbeat.

After a long ride to Butte, Montana, the Cards pull over at the Comfort Inn again for the night, but first, I'm taking the team out to a good meal at a good restaurant. I usually buy a good meal for the players after a long ride. Up and on the road again and we have around 380 more miles to cover, I-90 to I-94, and MC. Pete B. will face an old nemesis, the Pepsi-Challengers. Well-fed and rested, the Cards are successful, 6–2. Pete got a little help from David L. The same David allows five runs on five hits, going all the way for another Cardinal win, but that's it. We lose three in a row and go out with a whimper. The most exciting thing in MC was when Danny R. won $200 at the slots at the Town Pump. On several occasions throughout our times in MC, I've allowed players to take a vehicle to the ballpark while I stay "back at the ranch." Some players learned to take the back way, where they would speed up to cross the railroad tracks, splash into a puddle of water that was always there, and have to slam on their brakes to avoid landing in a neighbor's back yard. That was Miles City's Disneyland ride! I have to admit it, I tried it myself.

We are flying home on the thirteenth for a game on the fifteenth with Pomona. It's the last game of the regular season. Following that game we have two District Playoffs games. We are not successful in either games and finish the season with a six-game losing streak, but once again, as much as the players weren't happy about their performance on the field, their feelings were that what actually made the season was the road trip! I felt the same way.

THE TOUGHEST SEASON

The '98 season left little to cheer about, at home and on the road. We won three games on the road and eleven games at home out of forty-two games. Of the fourteen wins, Tim O. (4) and Josh L. (6) were our top pitchers, with a total of ten wins. The bright side of the season was three players who began with us last year as young rookies were back. All three claimed to be shortstops and played on the high school team. I liked all three as infielders and told them in their freshman year that they would make up our infield. It became my job to decide who would play where. After watching them play, I made the decision that the strongest arm, Justin B., would be the third baseman; the player with the best feet, Ben M., will play shortstop; and the quickest to catch and release the ball, Derek B., will play second base. One time, a parent questioned me about the importance of feet. He argued that Ben did not have a strong enough arm for shortstop. I told him that I thought Ben would get stronger and be able to make the throws. He did. The players seemed to be happy. I moved Eddie J. over to first base, rounding out a very good infield.

There was some exciting moments in the games before we hit the "happy trails." We opened the season with a 6–4 win in Ontario. Josh L. threw a four hitter, and Justin B., our third baseman, was three for three and had four RBIs. In the second game, Dave S. had a good four innings but was replaced by lefty Alex H. in his rookie debut. It wasn't pretty, as Alex gave up three runs on one hit and three walks. I mention Alex's uninspiring debut because you will hear from him later. Ontario beat us 4–1. We opened league play on a positive note, with a 10–7 win over Pomona. Derek B., our second baseman, had three hits and scored four times. Back-to-back ten runs, this time over La Verne, at home in the first game of a doubleheader, became very encouraging. Blake P. hit a towering 415-foot home run. In the second game, we managed only six hits but drew sixteen walks, with four La Verne errors, and scored twenty runs. We had a three-game winning streak, scoring forty runs! Make that four games and fifty-five runs. What an outburst! Matt R. had two home runs and five RBIs, and his brother Charles had one home run and three RBIs. Fireworks are over for several games, until Josh L. can pick up his fourth win over La Verne, 9–2. And then there was Charter Oak five days later.

Charter Oak had been in the league for several years, and we've had a good rapport with them. Josh was on the hill again and is spinning a nifty no-hitter into the sixth, but there is no score. Derek leads off with a double. Ben singles, Derek stops at third. A passed ball scores him for the Cards' first run. Danny R. singles, and Ben moves to third. Danny is one of our swiftest runners and takes off for second. Dan and Ben pull off a double-steal with Ben scoring. This is where it gets fun. Eddie follows with a double. He has been mouthing off to Charter Oak during the game. Alex pinch runs for him, and after he gets to third on a wild pitch, tries to score on another double steal, but is out at the plate, sliding in. When Alex H., who was running for loudmouth Eddie, stands up, the catcher coldcocks him, and a brawl ensues. The umpires break it up and toss several players out of the game. Charter Oak does not have enough players to finish the game, so they must forfeit to Claremont. Josh gets a no-hitter as Cards wins,

3–0. So much for the first game of a doubleheader. It's a seventeen to nine win in the second game, with Alex getting the win.

The Cards head out once again, this time for two games in Medicine Hat, Alberta. Claremont is 9–9 on the season. Ontario to Salt Lake to Billings to Med Hat, again. We will be missing two players, Matt and Charles R. After being late several times, not running out fly balls, and making up their own rules, they have decided to discontinue playing. Too bad, because they were two good athletes. Their dad got in the way. In two games in the "Hat," the Cards score three runs and allow twenty-three. Not a good start, but what it tells me is that our league at home is weak, considering all the runs we have scored. While in Medicine Hat, the Cards go out for a steak dinner at the Montana Steak House. Moving down Alberta 3 highway, to Lethbridge, again, Claremont will get ready for the tournament there. I have given a speech about the "ladies" and how we have had trouble keeping them out of rooms in the past. The Cards will play four teams in the tournament, all from Canada. Okanagan, Alberta, is first on the list. Josh does not finish the fourth inning, and we lose, 14–5. The Regina, Saskatchewan, Buffaloes are next, and we are more successful here as Tim O. goes all the way, 18–3. Derek is 3–3, with three RBIs. Calgary, Alberta, follows, and Steve B. gets his first win of the year, 10–3. After ninety-five pitches through five innings, he turns it over to Pete B. and Danny R. Lethbridge is next, and knocks us out of a possible championship with a 7–4 victory. Claremont, California, is two and two versus Canada! They head to Rapid City.

The Cardinals open up in Rapid City against a new foe, Dixon, Illinois. It was a wild high-scoring game, with the Cards dropping 11–10 when Josh gave up three straight hits in the last inning to allow Dixon to turn the game around. Tim O. faces Pueblo, Colorado, the next day and throws 107 pitches and allows eleven runs on twelve hits while the Cards score a scratch run on two hits. After two more losses, Claremont will face Casper, Wyoming, but the Cards are thin on pitching. Tim O. volunteers to start the game on the mound. He finishes it with a 3–1 win, allowing four hits. A total about-face for Tim.

The Cards' last two runs scored on back-to-back squeeze plays on two straight pitches. Nice, quiet Derek gets booted in the second inning. He tried to steal second base, was called out, and expressed his dismay. The Cardinals will take a trip up the hill to visit Mount Rushmore before the late game versus the hometown team. The inspiration did not carry over to the field with another loss. Casper, Wyoming, in the seventh place game, showed the same results. Gotta get outta town! We are heading to Miles City.

As it turned out, in Miles City, Claremont was the team to beat. And that is what happened. The Cards turned in their most dismal performances in the tournament, losing every game. Pete threw a decent game against Casper but lost. Garret hit his second home run of the year. The final road trip record was 3–16. Upon arrival back home, they had one more conference game and then playoffs. It has been quite obvious to me that our conference was mighty weak compared to what I saw on the road. Against Damien, at home, we had another high-scoring affair, scoring five runs in the bottom of the ninth to turn one around, 15–14. Every player who went to bat for us collected a hit, for nineteen hits. Eddie J. had four of them, including two doubles. Henry G.'s two-run RBI single was the game clincher. The Cards lost the first game of the District Playoffs. They won second game, which included the Claremont Cardinals' 12,000th hit, a single by Eddie J. in the second inning. The final game, versus Pomona, ended mercilessly, and appropriately, 18–3. That is not going to stop us. We will try it again next year.

THE LAST HURRAH!

It can only get better in the coming season—and it did. The one thing I knew entering the season was that our infield will be back. Justin, Ben, and Derek should make up a very strong, mature infield. Our first baseman for the past three years will be gone. Craig S. and Mahdy F. will take his place. Blake will be back in the outfield and in the middle of the lineup. We will add four new pitchers, and with what we have returning, we should be fine on the mound. Eric G., Damien G., Scott S., and Sean T. will be relied on heavily to bolster the staff. Added to the pitching staff was Scott S., who pitched for the CMC Stags. I'm hoping for a better showing than last season. I picked up the son of a very good friend of mine as an outfielder. Ted D. will keep our team thinking. He is quiet but "dangerous." You never knew what was on his mind. But he was fun to be around because something always happened! Ted and Sean are cousins, but completely different in demeanor.

The season will open with a conference game at Pomona. Alex H. gets the opening day assignment. Three runs are not enough. A four for five day, including a triple, by Ben M., our shortstop, is not enough, as

Pomona outscores us, 7–3. The Ontario Tournament is next. Damien makes his debut start for us. He struggles, and the Cards drop one to Ontario, 9–3. The Ontario pitcher had a no-hitter and shutout going into the sixth inning, but Ted breaks it up with a single.

That woke up the Cardinal hitters, and they put together a three-run inning, breaking up the shutout. Our first win comes against the Chino Reds, as the Cards broke loose for nineteen runs on nineteen hits, led by Ben's 3 for 3 day at the plate. Twelve players got hits, and Scott S. had four RBIs on two doubles. We dropped the consolation game to Alta Loma to end the tourney. The Cardinals start the season 1–5. Las Vegas Durango is coming to town. In the first game of a doubleheader, at Claremont McKenna College, Mike M. makes his first appearance on the mound for the Cardinals. Wow! What an appearance. Mike throws a four-hit shutout, and the Cards win, 1–0! In the second game, Alex isn't so lucky. We will start the trip with an 8–9 record.

This season, we begin the road trip in Las Vegas at Durango High School. The plan is to drive to Vegas, play the doubleheader, and then fly from Vegas to Billings. Parents will help us get to Vegas. The Cardinals received a large donation for the trip from an ex- player, Charlie, who played in '83. We stayed at Sam's Town. The temperature during the day rose to 112 degrees. By game time, it had gone down four degrees, so it was hot! The Cards were hot. In the first game, the Cardinal infielders, Justin, Ben, and Derek, had ten total hits in sixteen at bats. Derek was 4 for 4 with four RBIs. Ben's three hits were all doubles, and Justin had a triple. Scott threw a four-hit shutout. Cards should have saved something for the second game. Sean T. went all the way and gave up two runs on two hits, but Eddie's triple in the first wouldn't be enough, 2–1.

Flying out of Las Vegas is a first for the Cardinals. When you have to pay for eighteen tickets, you will save a little money when you can, and we did. We are loaded on the plane and rolling down the runway when the plane suddenly turns around. There will be a delay because of a particular malfunction. We are headed to Salt Lake City, where we are to make a connection to Billings, and then drive up to

Medicine Hat. We had reservations for the night at a motel in Havre, Montana. The flight delay lasted about an hour. When we finally got off of the ground, the flight to SLC was over an hour. Our connection was in another terminal, and we didn't have much time to make it. The entire team was sprinting to the next gate, E Gate. The connection to Billings was on a smaller plane, and the flight attendants had already placed two passengers that were on the waiting list, into our seats. After our sprint to the gate, the flight attendants had to go back on the plane and take those two passengers off of the plane, so that our entire team would be on the flight. They were very upset. We made it to Billings late. However, our luggage and equipment did not make it. We would have to wait for the next plane to come in from Salt Lake to get our luggage. That would be in about four hours. Holy moly! Delta gave us a $200 voucher for dinner. After picking up our ground transportation, I took the team to Perkins in Billings. Perkins was one of our favorite places to eat, if we could find one on the road. I called the motel in Havre to inform them that we'd be late coming in. After dinner, we went back to the airport, picked up our gear, and headed to Havre. By this time, it was after midnight. We drove north on US 87, through Roundup, Montana, through Grass Range, Montana, to a junction with US 191. I'm driving the lead vehicle and have two "navigators," Ted and Sean T., keeping me awake and checking maps to make sure we are headed in the right direction (at the time, GPS was not available). It's pitch dark as we get to a junction at Montana 66. We had made this trip a few years earlier, but I failed to recall which way we should go. The question is, do we stay on US 191 or take the junction? I recognized the town of Malta, so we stayed on US 191 to US 2. I make a left on US 2 and head to Havre, only to realize that we should have taken Montana 66. We will have to drive over fifty miles farther than we should have. Let Coach Brian B. (a player from the college where I coached) tell his story: "After a long flight, driving through the night from Billings, to Lethbridge, Canada, I didn't know what dark was, until being in the middle of Montana in the middle of the night. Before that trip, I knew Assistant Coach Helbs. During the trip, I got to know Head Coach Helbs. I received a baseball education in three weeks."

Eventually, the Cards make it to Havre at 4:00 a.m. The motel had an all-night desk clerk, so we checked in. There was no trouble getting the players to their rooms and to bed. Wake up will be at 11:00 a.m., allowing everyone seven hours of rest. Phew! The next morning, by noon, we head to Medicine Hat. The Cardinals drive north on Hill County road 232, out of Havre, to the Canadian border. At the border, the road becomes Alberta 41. Straight north to Trans-Canada 1, and left, to Medicine Hat.

Last year, at "The Hat," they bounced us in two games, 23–3. This year, in a single game, we returned the favor, scoring 15 runs and allowing 2! The game is scheduled for 7:00 p.m., so it is a day game. We opened the game with a triple by Justin and six runs in the first. Must have gotten a good rest in Havre. Alex, our resident lefty, finally showed what I knew he had with an excellent five-inning performance. Our classy infield turned in three double plays. We had a big lead, so I put Justin, our third baseman, on the hill to finish. Sean T. hit one out, and Justin, Derek, and Garret O. each tripled. The win makes the 165-kilometer trip on Alberta 3 to Lethbridge easy going. The Cards check into the motel across the street from Henderson Field. It used to be the Super 8 but has changed its name. On the same floor was a stripper. She invited the eligible ones to her show at a men's club, and they invited her to join them in five-pin bowling. In the first tournament game versus Twin Falls, Idaho, the Cards just keep on hitting, pitching, and playing great defense. The final score tells the story, 14–2. Eric L. was the benefactor on the mound. Justin, had three runs batted in. Game 2 sees us play a new team from a new province in Canada, Thompson, Manitoba. Consistent pitching, hitting, and defense carries us through another game. Two doubles and three runs batted in by Ben M. leads the way. Scott S. wins his third game. Claremont makes it four in a row with a 14–3 victory over Calgary. At the plate, Sean leads the way with three hits, and three runs batted in, and picks up the win on the hill. With an 8–6 victory over Medicine

Hat, the Cards make it five straight. Lethbridge ends the streak with a 8–1 victory. The Cards manage a lone single by Ben. Lethbridge has done well in the tourney, and this game simply takes both teams into the championship game. A great pitcher's duel ensues, with Scott S. allowing two runs on three hits, while his teammates can only earn one run on a scratch single by Ben. The Elks win the tournament.

The Cards head south to Rapid City. The plan is to stay at the Days Inn on the east end of town. They've been there before. When we pull up to the motel, something strange is apparent. No one else is booked into the motel, just us. They had a clerk at the front desk, so we went through all the motions of signing in. During the evening, something else is strange. There are no lights on the second floor, or any other floor but ours. It was eerie, as the players kept hearing noises from the upper floor. A few felt brave enough to go upstairs, but they didn't stay long. The players said the place was haunted and wanted to get out of there, which is what we did the next morning. I found a motel on the south side closer to the ballpark called the Kings Inn. They had enough rooms, if we would use a bay-type room that slept eight. I felt lucky that we could find something for all of us at such a short notice. We did. In the first game versus Dixon, Illinois, we score five runs in the first inning, five runs in the second inning, and seven runs in the third. Sean homered, Derek had four runs batted in, and Eric L. had three hits and three RBIs. That took time, and the game was called. Damien, Alex, and Justin each threw an inning, allowing two runs. Sean T. is pitching the next game against Pueblo, Colorado. He is starting to come into his own, as he allows one run on three hits, while the Cards are scoring eighteen runs on twenty hits. In the first two games in Rapid City, the Cards have scored thirty-five runs on thirty-six hits while allowing three runs on five hits. Before the Boulder, Colorado, game, which was scheduled for 2:30, I told the players that we'd be leaving about 1:15.

Your favorite shortstop, Ben M., comes to me and says, "Coach, I'll be a little late."

"What do you mean, you'll be late?"

"I have an appointment."

"Where?"

"Coach, I'm getting a perm."

What! Ben becomes the first player I have ever worked with who gets a perm. I said, "Okay," because I liked it. I have always liked an individual who had a personality, and Ben and his perm fit the mold. He comes back with his hair bulging out in curls, making it tougher to keep a cap on his head. This is one of my favorite stories.

More double-digit scoring against Boulder, Colorado, with Eric G. doing the pitching, 11–3. Eric helped himself with a three-for-three day at the plate. Leo chimed in with three RBIs. Against Denver, we scored ten, but Alex imploded on the hill and we lost, 13–11. Alex is going to be a good pitcher because he has a good selection of pitches. He walked five batters in two innings. I believe I could have done a better job in making sure he learned how to stay under control, but he has a tendency to be too emotional and excitable. Keep your eye on him, though. We go on and lose three more in a row, including the third place game against Boulder, Colorado. There were no fourth of July fireworks for us on that day. Prior to that game, earlier in the week, we went up the hill to view Mount Rushmore. At the museum on the grounds, Ted wandered around to see as much as he could and took a picture of himself with a simulated George Washington head.

We stayed another day in Rapid City to play their team again as a benefit game. The Cards were out of pitching, so Coach Darren W. was brought out of retirement. They "Boom Shaka laka'd" him for twelve hits, including three doubles and a triple and five walks, but he stuck it out, even when it took an extra inning. In the last inning, the Cardinals scored two runs on a double by Blake and a single by Sean to win, 9–8. Derek, our slick fielding second baseman, hits his only home run of the year, a two-run shot to left. With a fireworks stop on the road in the boonies of Montana, we're off to Miles City.

The Miles City tournament is always a tough tourney. They bring in some great teams and try not to have any other Montana teams in the tournament, so if you do well, it's great for your team's psyche. Eric throws a complete game in the opener against an old foe, the Eugene Pepsi-Challengers, and gets help from Ben M.'s home run to escape, 8–7. Sean keeps it going with a four hitter and a 4–1 game over the hometown team. After the game, the Cards are hosted by the locals, down the left field line to a pitchfork fondue. Only two teams were invited to the steak fry, Miles City and Claremont. Members of other teams were chased away by the local fans. Jamestown, North Dakota, stops us in our tracks with a 4–1 win in a game where Sean T. is injured running the bases and is out for the rest of the season.

Back on track versus Yakima, Washington. Although it wasn't a well-played game, Scott S. escapes a nine-run second inning, while the Cards finally out score Yakima with a run in the sixth on Justin's fourth RBI of the game, 13–12. Mahdi's three-run home run in the first got the Cards started. Despite Scott S.'s and Sean H's home runs, the Cards drop one to El Segundo. Scott's was his first life time homer. He needs to work on his home run trot. The pitchers for that game were our third baseman, Justin; our shortstop, Ben; and our second baseman, Derek. Justin, our diminutive third baseman, is the starting pitcher, and in the first inning, their third hitter, Alberto, hits a three-run jack. Let Justin tell the story: "The next time he came up, I gave him my best heater into his back, and he thought about charging me and I told him to bring it on, and he backed off. He was bigger than me, but didn't have the (courage). All the while, his pops, a major leaguer with the Padres, is yelling in the stands that it was bush league."

Knowing we will be in the semis tomorrow, the main staff gets the day off. Eric G. responds with a complete game victory over Eugene, Oregon, 11–6, sparked by a home run by Blake. Scott S. can't get out of the first inning in the championship game, and the Cards can't muster any major attack, and we fall, 9–2, in the championship game with El Segundo. Craig, Ben, Sean T., Mahdi, Blake all make the all-tournament team. Overall, it was a good showing for the Cardinals. They go home to face District Playoffs. The 16–6 and 16–8 losses end the season for the 1999 Claremont Cardinals. They finish the season with a 21–22 record and 12–12 on the road. It has been a great three years with the three infielders. They became the backbone of the team, both physically, and mentally. Derek B. set an all-time team record with a .974 fielding average, making only four errors this season. Derek, .381; Ben, .376; and Justin, .342 bolstered the lineup all season long. I have had so much pleasure working with those three and feel the decisions made on which position they should play was absolutely correct.

In 1980, there was never a plan to travel with the Claremont Cardinals' American Legion team, on the road for twenty years. What occurred was each year, because of the last season, I decided to do it again, and again, and again. Many things happened, but we overcame any problems. I never had to bail a player out of jail or face any serious felonious situations. As a matter of fact, I preached every year to our players, "The players before you had established a great reputation, so don't do anything to ruin that reputation for the next group of players." While we were in Miles City, I had bragged that I had retired from never working a day in my life. In June of 1999, I retired from thirty years of teaching and coaching, so when the summer season began, I had no more connection with Claremont High School. Consequently, the Claremont Cardinals' experience had played out. It was very sad for me, because in the end, I loved the team, the players, and something from every season. I'm happy that I was able to provide our local young baseball players "a summer to remember!" However, for me, I know there is a future.

WHAT TO DO
OFF THE FIELD

It's easy to take care of your players on the field, but as you can see, a big problem is what to do off of the field. Besides playing acey deucey cards in the room, watching ball games or movies on the tube, I needed a team activity around town. I came up with the Summer Games. Gather the players together and let them divide themselves up into four teams. Any one leftover would be on the coaches' team. One night, I would go to a pool hall and ask to rent two tables for a couple of hours for the team. Usually the answer was okay, but no drinking alcohol, a given. The players would follow a schedule where every team would play each other, and the team with the most wins would be recorded. Another time, I would find a three-par golf course and rent the clubs for each team, and we would have a golf tournament. We staggered the tee-offs. The lowest scores would be recorded and added with the pool scores. On a third night, we'd be at a bowling alley, and the same procedure would take place. Finally, one or two other ideas would occur. I had a list of several baseball trivia questions, and we'd put that to use.

One day, in Lethbridge, it was pouring rain, so I went to the local YMCA and booked two hours of time on the basketball courts. The teams would have to play a round-robin and we'd record the place of finishing. At the end, I totaled everything up and determined the winning team. After the season was over, at our last team get-together, I would have T-shirts made with the year and "Cardinal Summer Games Champs." The Summer Games became fun and competitive. DQ, anyone? That was a popular call on some nights. I would usually get ten to twelve takers for a trip to the local Dairy Queen for ice cream, always on the me through team money. Off the field. We played a lot of whiffle ball, sometimes into the night. Fishing was popular with several players, and I'd make sure they had transportation to the river or lake nearby. Only a few jumped off the Paragon Bridge in Miles City. A Paragon bridge was usually constructed with old railroad flat cars.

MEDICAL CARE

While on the road for twenty years, we could not escape possible injuries in a game or while traveling. Besides Rob P.'s homesickness, which was cured by time, we had a broken collarbone in Lethbridge. It was an afternoon game on a Saturday, and we took the player to the hospital after the game. I can report that a hospital visit in Canada on a Saturday night is much quieter than a Saturday night trip to the hospital in Southern California. In a game in Miles City, our catcher was hit in the head by a back swing by the hitter and spent two days in the hospital there. Cedric's broken thumb called for a trip to the hospital where it was set and otherwise taken care of. Also, in Miles City, Danny R. was sprinting to first base and stretched out to reach the bag and hyper-extended his knee, which put him into the hospital and out for the rest of the season. Of course, I mentioned earlier, Randy R.'s wiped-out knee in Yountville at State Playoffs. Amazingly, our major accident in North Dakota did not cause any major injuries. One catcher had wrenched his back a little, but that didn't last long. That is about it. I feel very lucky that we had no real dangerous, life-threatening events in those twenty years.

MILES CITY, MONTANA

Back in June of the school year, I applied for retirement after thirty years of teaching. When the summer season began, I was no longer a teacher at Claremont High School. While we were in Miles City, I had bragged that I had retired from "never working a day in my life." Later in the year, about September, I got a call asking if I'd be interested in coaching the Miles City Mavericks. Their coach had resigned. I told the caller that I'd have to think about it and I'd like to talk to the coach that resigned. The coach gave me the green light and wished me well. I took the job. I was told to bring my program from Claremont up to Miles City. In November, the board flew me to Billings and Miles City for an introduction meeting with the parents and players. It was at the Cellar Lounge, a great pizza place, among other things. We had a good meeting, as I gave my introduction spiel. After talking about my program, I opened it up to questions. The very first question from a player, came from Kelly M., and it set me back a little. "Will we be doing the phantom infield?" What? the phantom infield that the Cardinals had put on a couple of times in Miles City.

I knew that it had been a hit, but never expected that it would be the most important question of the night. "Absolutely!"

I brought with me an assistant coach who had played in high school and on the Legion team, Darren W. I also kept a pitching coach from the past season, Eric H., for some continuity. After our first workout, Coach Darren and I went to the Cellar Lounge for pizza and to compare notes. We looked at each other, and both of us shook our heads, expressing that we've got work to do.

The first few months in Miles City was a great cultural lesson for a Southern California boy. After the first day of practice, I watched a young thirteen-to-fourteen-year-old player leave the ballpark, climb into the cab of an F-350, in the driver's seat, reach up behind the sun visor, and grab a can of snoose (snuff to you), tap it twice, take a pinch, and drive away!

Early in the season, in May, I told the players on a Friday that we'd be practicing on Saturday at ten o'clock. Kevin R. raised his hand and said, "Coach, I won't be at practice tomorrow."

"Why not?"

"My dad is the foreman on a ranch in Terry, and we are branding cattle tomorrow. I have to help because it is a family business."

My mind is wheeling, but I can't battle this situation, so I excused him from practice. One time on a bus ride, I got up and went to the back of the bus to listen to the music that was playing on a boom box they had. They were playing a Garth Brooks album and knew every word of very song. I like country music too, but maybe not that deep. On my way back to my seat, I passed a fifteen-year-old rookie who we all dubbed "Rube." He was thumbing through a *Playboy* magazine. I felt better. Some things were still normal.

Mac tells this story, "First day with the big shot coach from California, and he has the infielders go hit and the outfielders do some drills, so I'm in the outfield. Then he swaps, so I'm in the infield with more drills. He then says, 'Catcher's drills, and if you haven't hit, get some hitting in.' He sees me at the catcher's drills, looks at me, and says, 'You're freaking here too? I remember these small town teams have to have someone who can play more than one position.' After practice, with no BP, he asks what position I played last year. I told him, 'All of them except pitcher and first base.' A few days later, he called me over and told me that I was going to be the second baseman. 'Right now, you are not very good, but we will change that.'"

I'll never forget the moment when I told him that. The anguish, anxiety he had about making the team was immediately released with a huge deep breath. Several days later, we are playing in Gillette, Wyoming, with Tyrel G. pitching a great game, no hits into the fifth. In the bottom of Gillette's fifth inning, a hitter pops up to shallow right field, behind the first baseman. The right fielder comes in, first baseman backs up, and Mac angles over for the catch. They all look at each other, and the ball falls in for a hit—the only hit that Tyrel allows. When Mac comes into the dugout, I approached him (read accosted) and let him know that for the rest of the year, he is to catch any pop fly he can get to. After the season was over, I went through the score books and counted all the pop ups he caught after the Gillette game. The total was fifty-two. Mac turned into an excellent second baseman with a very quick release on a double play turn. As an infield coach, I was excited about his progress. We developed a very good relationship, alive today. My first year, 2000, I scheduled a road trip, ala Claremont, without the plane flight. The Mavericks traveled in their own bus with their own driver. I called it "The Western Swing." The Mavs played in Missoula, Whitefish, and in a tournament in Kalispell. In 2001 and 2002, we went to the college world series in Omaha, Nebraska. Both trips were exciting, watching the best college players. We went on the first weekend, so that we could see all the teams play, but that meant we would not see the finals the following weekend. In 2001, I also scheduled us into a tournament, whereby we would play in the morning and go to the tournament in the afternoon. I didn't like that, so the following year, we did not play in the tournament, and instead saw all the games on that weekend. Miles City was great for me and my Claremont teams through the years, and I was excited to have the opportunity to coach at Miles City. I was there for three years, and I will admit, they were all fun years. The 2001 team ranks in my top five fun teams to have been associated with. I can list them in order, but not in these pages.

That year, the Mavs won the Newhouse for the first and only time. On the season, we were 57–24. Later, Kelly, my first captain, had become head coach in Libby and hired me as an assistant, for eleven seasons. I am grateful to have been able to associate with these players: Mac, who worked hard and became a very efficient second baseman; Andy, who struggled the first season and made a great return the next; Chase, a great fly chaser who roamed Death Valley; Tyrel G. and Tyler C., our bomb squad; and Tyler L, who found first base as a position he liked; Kevin R., our resident wrangler; Rube, who subscribed to *Playboy* magazine and was a great pitcher for us; Jake, who played right field with one arm very efficiently; Tony, who took our guys fishing several years ago, Andrew R., who when he was in the game it was crunch time; Brad, a serious fisherman himself; Matt C., an imposing pitcher; Andy P., the son of the past coach; Rafe, our lefty; Ace B., who told me the following year that he wasn't going to play because he was going to join the rodeo circuit, all made the seasons memorable for me. In 2001, we hit fifty home runs as a team. Long live Electric Avenue! My time in Miles City is for another book.

1981 Claremont Cards Going to State

1982 Claremont Cardinals at Madison River

1983 Cards in Las Vegas

1984 Claremont Cards at Grand Tetons Wyo.

1985 Cards at Mt. Rushmore

1986 Claremont Cards at Tower Falls

1986 Claremont Cards on Snake River

1988 Cards at Glacier National Park

1989 at Lethbridge Alb.

1990 Claremont Cards on Gallatan River

1991 Claremont Cards at Roughlock Falls, SD.

1992 Cards at Montana Bar

1993 Claremont Cards MC Champs

1994 Cards at Yellowstone

1996 Claremont Cardinals at Lake Louise Banff

1999 Cardinals at Miles City

Ben's Perm

Bill W. and The Boys in the Stands at Denton

Boyz at Custers Place

Calgary Stampede

Camp Cook '96

Canoe Races at Miles City

Cardinal Transportation 1983

Cardinals 1999 Newhouse Miles City Tour.

Cemetary at Little Big Horn Battlefield

Centerfield Flag Pole at Denton

Cliff and Danny on the Columbia July 4, '95

In Between Games 1994

Lake Louise Banff Alb

Liu C. and Lou D.

Miniature Golfing

North Dakota-Lazin' on the Ol' Missouri

Oakland 1988 State Playoffs

Smokeout '98

The Corral Gardiner Montana

Welcome Home!

Players' Comments

"Jack is one of the most passionate coaches I have ever known. He is a player's coach and his knowledge of the game is phenomenal."

—Charlie Reynoso, President,
Inland Valley Baseball

"The Legion trips you put together for us are some of the best baseball memories I have. Fireworks, 8 men to a room, beating pretty much everyone."

"The game against El Segundo is the most fun I ever had pitching."

—Matt W.

"I threw my best amateur games for Helbs."

—Sean T.

"Celebrate your antics, poke fun at yourself, while humbly admitting that you profoundly touched the lives of thousands of young men."

—Sheri B.

"We were good because of the confidence and skill set you instilled in us."

—Justin B.

"I enjoyed you as a coach, Helbs. The best times I ever had was on the field. Lots of teams out there didn't get as lucky."

—Dylon L.

"Not for the craziness of the road trips, but to see history. Mt. Rushmore, Custer's battlefield, the barely started Crazy Horse monument. Just seeing the parts of the country that SoCal guys wouldn't necessarily get to see. For that, I thank you."

—Jeff S.

"Some of the most fun and best summers of my life."

—Tyler C.

"Written by one of the most passionate and knowledgeable baseball coaches out there."

—Keith Prager, former MLB scout
for Boston Red Sox/current
High School Coach

Numbers

In twenty years on the road, The Claremont Cardinals played 357 games. The overall record was 223–134 for a .625 win percentage. Approximately, 213 players from three high schools and one college participated in the Cardinal road trips. During those years, the Cards played 81 different teams from 19 different states, 4 countries. The countries included the United States, Canada, Taiwan, and Australia. The states included:

From California: Manhattan Beach, Aurora, Santa Maria, Orcutt, Albany, Lafayette, Union City, Lodi, Lompoc, El Segundo, Merced, Antelope Valley

From Colorado: Boulder, Colorado Springs, Denver, Grand Junction, Littleton, Pueblo

From Idaho: Blackfoot, Boise, Idaho Falls, Klamath Falls, Pocatello, Twin Falls

From Illinois: Dixon

From Kansas: Manhattan

From Michigan: Escanaba, Hancock

From Minnesota: Burnsville, Eden Prairie, Moorhead, Waite Park

From Montana: Billings (two teams), Great Falls (two teams), Miles City.

From Nebraska: Scottsbluff

From Nevada: Las Vegas (three teams)

From New Mexico: Albuquerque

From North Dakota: Bismarck, Fargo, Jamestown, Minot, Williston

From Oregon: Bend, Eugene, Portland,

From South Dakota: Rapid City, Sioux Falls, Sturgis

From Texas: Dallas, Galena Park

From Utah: Bonneville, Brigham City, Hillcrest, Holladay, Ogden, Roy, Salt Lake, Taylorsville

From Washington: Bellevue, Clarkston, Ephrata, Kennewick, Pasco, Seattle, Spokane, Yakima
From Wisconsin: Eau Claire
From Wyoming: Casper, Cody, Laramie, Sheridan

From Alberta: Calgary, Fort Saskatchewan, Lethbridge, Okanagan
From British Columbia: Trail
From Manitoba: Thompson
From Saskatchewan: Regina

In twenty years, the Cardinals participated in 60 tournaments in 16 towns and won 24 of them.

Major League Players: Mark McGwire (A's, Cardinals), Matt Wise (Angels, Brewers), Sean Tracey, (White Sox, Orioles), and Alex Hinshaw (Giants)

In memoriam:

Robert Skapik
1972–1994
Pitcher, first baseman, outfielder for the Cardinals in 1987, 1989–90.

ABOUT THE AUTHOR

The author has coached baseball on several levels in sixty seasons. Sometimes, two teams a year, being spring ball, and then summer baseball. He has coached at several levels beginning on the youth level of fifteen- and sixteen-year-old players in 1960. After graduating from high school in 1958, he attended California Polytechnic College (now a university), and after two years, he was drafted into the US Army. After training, he spent two years as a meteorologist at Fort Sill, Oklahoma. He returned to Cal Poly following his army duty and graduated in 1968 with a major in physical education and a minor in history. His first professional coaching job was Marshall Junior High School in Pomona, California. From there, he received an offer to teach at his alma mater, Claremont High School, in California. After six years as the head junior varsity baseball coach, he was offered the head coaching position as varsity baseball coach. From 1972–1985, he coached varsity baseball, and in 1972, he started a summer program in conjunction with the American Legion and called the team the Claremont Cardinals. In the 1978–79 summer seasons, the Cardinals entered a tournament in Santa Maria, California. In actuality, this was the first experience in traveling on the road and staying overnight for the team. This became a spark for a more extensive road trip. To fan that spark, a cousin of the author had invited him to a Little League Regional playoff game in San Bernardino, California, to watch his little brother Pete, play for Laramie, Wyoming. In conversations, it was brought up that maybe the Claremont team could possibly come to a tournament in Laramie in the Summer of 1980. From August of 1979 to the beginning of 1980, this thought burned in the mind of the author, who finally succumbed to it and got back to his cousin Paul, and they made arrangements for Claremont to enter the Laramie Tournament. The rest is history, documented in these pages.

Coach Helber left the Claremont Varsity baseball program in 1986 when he was invited by his college coach, John Scolinos, to become an assistant coach at California Polytechnic College. After spending two years at Cal Poly, he received a call from the head coach at Claremont McKenna College, Randy Town, asking if he'd be interested in assisting at CMC. He took the job and spent twenty-three years as assistant baseball coach at CMC. Coach Jack Helber has been a member of the American Baseball Coaches Association since 1986 and has written a book entitled *Baseball Psychology, The Gray Matter Factor*, with a second edition captioned, *The Second Inning*.

This book, *Have Bats, Will Travel*, chronicles the twenty years that the Claremont Cardinals American Legion baseball team traveled. Every story is true, and every player's name is real, although, because of security reasons and ex-players' privacy, only their first name is used. No player's last name is listed. No story has been fabricated or embellished. The author hopes that in reading this book, you get a sense of the excitement and enjoyment that each person who had the opportunity to participate received.